# LEARNING
# AND
# LIVING

## John Blanchard

HENRY WALTER LTD

First published in 1975 by
H. E. Walter Ltd
26 Grafton Road, Worthing
West Sussex BN11 1QU, England

This second revised edition
published in 1979

ISBN 0 85479 541 3

*Printed in Great Britain by
Hazell Watson & Viney Ltd
Aylesbury, Bucks*

# Contents

|  | Page |
|---|---|
| Explanation | vii |
| Foreword | ix |
| Introduction | xi |

*LEARNING THE CHRISTIAN LIFE*

| One — Why do I need God? | 3 |
|---|---|
| 1. Sin | 3 |
| 2. Guilt | 8 |

| Two — How can I find God? | 13 |
|---|---|
| 3. New Birth | 13 |
| 4. Repentance | 20 |
| 5. Faith | 27 |

| Three — What does God offer me? | 33 |
|---|---|
| 6. Justification | 33 |
| 7. Adoption | 41 |
| 8. Assurance | 50 |

*LIVING THE CHRISTIAN LIFE*

| Four — Pleasing my Father | 59 |
|---|---|
| 9. Sanctification | 59 |
| 10. Service | 69 |
| 11. Watchfulness | 80 |

|  |  | *Page* |
|---|---|---|
| Five — Fighting my enemy |  | 91 |
| 12. | The Devil | 91 |
| 13. | Temptation | 100 |
| Six — Following my Saviour |  | 111 |
| 14. | Fruitbearing | 111 |
| 15. | Witnessing | 122 |
| Seven — Doing my duty |  | 133 |
| 16. | The Holy Spirit | 133 |
| 17. | The Will of God | 146 |
| Eight — Enjoying my fellowship |  | 157 |
| 18. | The Bible | 157 |
| 19. | Prayer | 164 |
| 20. | The Church | 177 |

# Explanation

For a book to have two joint authors is not unusual — but when one of them is living in heaven and the other on earth, the situation is a little different: so perhaps a word of explanation is necessary!

My colleagues and I in the Movement for World Evangelization are firm believers in the ministry of good Christian literature, and for some time now we have felt it to be an important part of our work to commend to people, both inside and outside of the Christian church, books which we believe will be of real value to them. Some time ago, we came across a book which seemed about to sink into oblivion after four editions spread over a period of 23 years. The title of the book was *Learning and Living the Christian Life,* and the author the Rev. G. R. Harding Wood. The style was simple, the structure attractive, and the contents helpful, and we soon found that young and old, in faith and years, were buying it on our recommendation and finding it a useful guideline in framing the basics of Christian faith and conduct.

As the last edition of the book began to run out, I discussed with my colleagues an idea that had been moving towards the front of my mind as I re-read its pages: *shouldn't this book be re-written?* This would given an opportunity to amplify it, modernise the phraseology, take advantage of modern Bible translation and generally up-date the presentation, whilst maintaining the basic outline of the book. With their encouragement, I discussed this with the publishers and was delighted at their immediate and whole-hearted endorsement of the idea. Carrying it out has been a delightful experience and I sincerely hope that at the end of the day we have something that will prove of real value to all who read these pages.

I would like to express my particular appreciation to Mrs. Maureen Vellacott, Mr. Wood's beneficiary, for her happy agreement to the book being re-written, to The Bishop of Norwich for his kind Foreword, to Ian Walter for his encouragement and help throughout the project, and last but not least to my wife, who filtered the typing of the manuscript into her full-time ministry as wife and mother in the Blanchard household.

I trust that 'Uncle Harding' – as he was known to so many people – will approve of what I have done, even though only the barest traces of the original can now be found. Perhaps we can discuss it when we meet, and as there is no dissension of any kind in heaven, I can only assume that his agreement to this new arrangement of his original theme will be as perfect as my explanation of why I felt it necessary!

Croydon, Surrey.        JOHN BLANCHARD

**NOTE:**
In revising this book for its second edition, I have re-worded many of the Bible references, so that they are now all taken direct from one uniform translation, *The New International Version.* Of the numerous English translations now available, the NIV may well prove to be the finest of all, and I hope that its use here will encourage Christians to read it through and test it for themselves. I have also shortened the title to that by which it has become popularly known – *Learning and Living.*

# Foreword
## to the first edition

---

by The Right Rev. Maurice A. P. Wood, D.S.C., M.A.,
R.N.R., Bishop of Norwich

I am very happy to write this Foreword to *Learning and Living the Christian Life,* which was originally written by my uncle, The Rev. G. R. Harding Wood, and has now been produced in its modern and revised form by John Blanchard of the Movement for World Evangelization, whom I have known for many years.

It has been my very great privilege to be brought up in a family that has believed whole-heartedly in evangelism, and has emphasised that warmth of the heart and understanding of the mind lead to commitment of the will to Jesus Christ and to his service. I can still hear my uncle's clear thought and apposite illustrations coming freshly to me from this book, and John Blanchard has done his work of revision, expansion and modernization with delicacy, insight, humour and equal clarity.

I write this Foreword in the Centenary Year of the great Keswick Convention, at which my father, Arthur Wood, and my uncles all heard their call to whole-time Christian ministry. My prayer is that this new presentation of *Learning and Living the Christian Life* will help many young people and others to put their trust in Jesus Christ as their Saviour, and to commit themselves whole-heartedly to him as their Lord and Master.

I am delighted to know that this book will be reaching a new generation and a wider public, and I wish it well.

MAURICE NORVIC:

# Introduction

Many people today are confused about what it is to become a Christian, and what it means to live as a Christian in today's world. Perhaps that is not too surprising, because there are so many extravagant and eccentric things being said and done within the Christian church, and so many cults, sects and 'isms' on the fringes of it, that it must at times be very difficult for the interested non-Christian or the relative beginner in the faith to separate the wood from the trees.

All of this means that there has never been a greater need than now to get *back to basics,* which in Christian things means getting *back to the Bible,* and it is to help people to do that that this book has been written. In his letter to the early church at Colosse, the Apostle Paul said 'we have not stopped praying for you and asking God to fill you with the knowledge of his will through all spiritual wisdom and understanding' (Colossians 1:9), and he then went on to speak of his longing that all the Christians to whom he wrote might have *'the full riches of complete understanding'* (Colossians 2:2). That is a great phrase! To understand spiritual truth, and to be sure of understanding it, is to make a person a spiritual millionaire — but the tragedy today is that so many people in and around the church are so doctrinally impoverished that they would qualify for supplementary benefit if such a thing were available!

It is because I am so concerned about this that I have taken the very unusual step in this particular book of not including a single quotation from any other source but the Bible. Of course it would be very interesting to use statements made by theologians and thinkers soldiers and scientists, poets and pop stars, artists and authors; and I could easily have included sayings from scores of people from Socrates to Solzhenitsyn. But I have deliberately ignored them all. Instead, I have built the whole book around nearly 600 quotations from the Bible, so that the truth of its teaching rests not on even the finest statements of even the greatest of men, but on 'the living and enduring word of God' (1 Peter 1:23).

In Christian doctrine, as in any other subject, there are certain words that are somewhat technical, and therefore need careful explaining, especially to those outside, or only just inside, the Christian church. The first part of this book will concentrate on doing just that, in the belief that understanding leads to assurance, and that assurance in turn leads to joy, liberty and effectiveness. In the second part of the book we shall turn to the question of day to day Christian living, but we will still do so with an open Bible before us at every point, for the simple reason that 'All scripture is God-breathed and is useful for teaching, rebuking, correcting and training in righteousness, so that the man of God may be thoroughly equipped for every good work' (2 Timothy 3:16—17). No words of mine could more perfectly sum up the whole purpose of the book you are now reading.

# LEARNING THE CHRISTIAN LIFE

# One — Why do I need God?

---

## 1. SIN

To answer this fundamental question, we need to begin at the beginning. The Bible tells us that when God had finished his great work of creation, he was able to look upon it all and pronounce 'it was very good' (Genesis 1:31). The whole universe, from the mightiest galaxy to the smallest organism, was perfect in God's sight, and this perfection included man, made 'in the image of God' (Genesis 1:27). Even in the judgment of a perfectly righteous and all-wise Creator, there was not even the smallest blemish to be found anywhere in the universe.

### Something went wrong

One does not have to be a theological genius, a highly trained social observer, or even remotely religious, to agree that things are not like that now! Things have changed — and the cause of the fantastic revolution that took place in the universe can be summed up in one biblical word — 'sin'. When man chose to disobey God, and go his own way, not only was his own relationship with God broken, but the whole universe was put out of joint. As far as man himself is concerned, the Bible could not be more straightforward about it — 'your iniquities have separated you from your God; your sins have hidden his face from you, so that he will not hear' (Isaiah 59:2).

To understand just what this means, we have to look a little more closely at the three major words the Bible uses for wrongdoing. These are 'sin', 'trangression' and 'iniquity'. Let us take a closer look at each of these words in turn, because the better our understanding of the nature of sin, the clearer our understanding of why man needs God.

## Missing the mark

To put it as simply as possible, the word 'sin' means missing the mark, or failing to meet God's standard. The Bible says that 'all have sinned and fall short of the glory of God' (Romans 3:23), and the second part of the phrase helps to explain the first part. When the Bible says that all men are sinners, it means that all men, even the best of them, are less than perfect in God's pure sight, and are therefore moral and spiritual failures. What is more, the Bible also teaches that man sins *because he is a sinner by nature.* Even as a mature Christian, the Apostle Paul had to admit, 'I know that nothing good lives in me, that is, in my sinful nature' (Romans 7:18). The theological expression for this is 'total depravity', which does not mean that every man is as sinful as it is possible for a person to be, but that every part of his personality is affected by the sinfulness of his nature. A watch may be shockproof, waterproof, automatic, 24 carat gold and bursting with jewels, but if the mainspring is broken it is useless; and however hard he tries, man is just as useless when it comes to reaching God's standard, or fulfilling his purpose. No amount of education or sophistication can alter the simple truth that man is a sinner, born with a fatal inability to hit the target God has set for him.

## Overstepping the line

The meaning of our second word gives us a contrasting picture. Whereas sin is failing to come up to the mark, transgression means overstepping the line. In the course of a long discussion about man's failure Paul says that 'where there is no law there is no transgression' (Romans 4:15) — which means, of course, that the opposite is also true, namely, that where there *is* law there *is* transgression. If I see a 'No Parking' sign and deliberately leave my car in that part of the road, I am guilty of transgression, I have broken the law. What the Bible teaches is that to know what is right and to do what is wrong is transgression, something of which we are all guilty, without exception and without excuse.

## The fatal bias

There is a sense in which perhaps we should have looked at the word 'iniquity' first, because in one way it is the root of both sin and transgression. The word means 'in-equity'; it is a lack of balance, or a fatal bias, in human nature, and one that is true of every man. Even the mighty King David confessed 'Surely I have been a sinner from birth, sinful from the time my mother conceived me' (Psalm 51:5). No father has to teach his child to lie, steal, cheat, or lose his temper. All of these things come *naturally,* because the child has been 'a sinner from birth'.

## The stories Jesus told

In Luke 15, Jesus told three stories which further illustrate the words we have been studying.

*The lost silver is a picture of sin (vv. 8—10).* The coin concerned was lost *helplessly.* There was nothing it could do to get itself found. The Bible tells us bluntly that 'Those controlled by their sinful nature cannot please God' (Romans 8:8) and that left to himself, man is 'dead in . . . transgressions and sins' (Ephesians 2:1). What is more, we are told that 'The man without the Spirit does not accept the things that come from the Spirit of God, for they are foolishness to him and he cannot understand them, because they are spiritually discerned' (1 Corinthians 2:14). In plain language, man is as helpless to find God as was that lost coin to find its owner.

*The lost son is a picture of transgression (vv. 11–32).* The younger son was lost *wilfully*. He deliberately chose to go his own way, 'do his own thing', run his own life; and the Bible speaks of men who 'leave the straight paths to walk in dark ways, who delight in doing wrong and rejoice in the perverseness of evil' (Proverbs 2:13–14).

*The lost sheep is a picture of iniquity (vv. 3–7).* The sheep was lost *naturally*. It is in the very nature of sheep to wander, to stray, to get lost; and the Bible says 'We all, like sheep, have gone astray, each of us has turned to his own way' (Isaiah 53:6). Just as a sheep is a wanderer by nature, so man is a sinner by nature.

All of this is a long way from the man in the street's conception of sin. To some people, it is limited to things like murder or adultery; to others, it is just a theological idea, or 'something invented by the church'. But when we turn to the Bible we see sin in its true colours. It is described as a stain, a rebellion, a poison, crookedness, a burden, a storm, wandering, a sickness, a disease, a field of weeds, darkness, blindness, bondage, a debt, robbery and a curse. Sin is not trivial, but terrible. Sin is not superficial, it is something deep-rooted in the human heart. Sin is not a psychological idea, it is a spiritual fact. Sin is not a toy, it is a killer. Sin brought God's curse on the devil and on man, it scarred the ecology of the whole universe, it killed the Lord Jesus Christ, and it separates men from God.

## Have you got the message?

It was in the Garden of Eden that the devil began the business of temptation by minimising the nature and the gravity of sin. He was so successful then that he has not needed to change his tactics since. There is no surer way to prevent a sick man from going to the doctor than to persuade him that he is physically fit: and the devil is still busy persuading people that, spiritually speaking, they need no radical treatment. Now to be suffering from a major disease is serious, but to be suffering from that same disease and not to know it is a double tragedy, because the man in that position will do nothing to have the disease cured. When a man does not realise that he was born with a spiritual disease for which there is no human cure, that that disease affects every part of his personality, and that unless something is done that same disease will separate him from God for ever, then he is in a desperate condition indeed! This paraphrase of Romans 7:9 gives an idea of how the truth of his position came home to Paul — 'There was once a time when I fancied that I was all right . . . then God's law was brought home to my conscience, and the sense of sin woke up, and I saw that in the sight of God I was dead'. Have you grasped that message? Have you ever realised that you are a sinner by birth, by nature, by habit and by choice, and that left in that condition you are 'without hope and without God in the world' (Ephesians 2:12)?

If you are a Christian, then you will have already come to that conclusion, and will have found the answer to the dilemma and disaster of sin. But if you are not a Christian, and have never before realised just how serious sin is, then ask God *now* to give you a deep, personal sense of the reality and result of sin, and, as you read on, to show you his wonderful solution to your problem!

## 2. GUILT

If a prison inmate were to tell you the story of how he came to be there, certain factors would follow in natural order — sin, guilt, condemnation and punishment. As soon as the crime had been committed, he became guilty. Later, when his case was heard in court, he was condemned. Now, he is suffering punishment. The same order is true spiritually — sin, guilt, condemnation and punishment. But whereas a crime is an offence against the law of man, sin is an offence against the law of God, with the result that the guilt, condemnation and punishment are all much more serious.

### How do I fit into Genesis?

To say that sin brings guilt raises no problem. If I deliberately choose to disobey God, then of course I am guilty, whether I feel it or not. But the Bible says that we are sinners by nature, that is that we are born sinners. In Paul's own words, 'the result of one trespass was condemnation for all men' (Romans 5:18). What does this mean? Is guilt universal? Are *we* guilty because *Adam* sinned? Surely God cannot hold us responsible for the sin of our first parents, and condemn and punish us as a result of *their* disobedience?

And if God cannot do that, when does personal guilt begin, and how does it operate? Was David really right to say 'I have been a sinner from birth, sinful from the time my mother conceived me'? Surely a man is not guilty in God's sight *before* he commits his first sin?

To unravel those questions, we need to have a clear understanding of what happened when Adam first sinned — the event which theologians call 'the Fall'. God created Adam perfect and innocent, and put him into the Garden of Eden with a free will. He was capable of choosing between good and evil, right and wrong, and for some time — we are not told how long — Adam and his wife Eve constantly chose to obey God, to do right, with the result that they lived in perfect harmony, not only with each other, but with their Maker. Then, in the way we have described for us in Genesis 3, the moment came when for the first time Adam and Eve said 'No' to God and 'Yes' to the devil. In that moment, man lost his unique and perfect relationship with God. He was no longer a perfect son, but a polluted sinner. His natural inclination to do good was replaced by a natural inclination to do evil. He developed an appetite for sin. He lost his moral balance. And all of these things — sinnership, a natural bias toward sin, and an appetite for sin, or loss of moral balance, were transmitted by Adam to the whole human race, of which he was the head. He was not only the natural head of the human race, he was the responsible head. When he sinned, he did so as man's representative, and when he had children, they were born 'in his own likeness, in his own image' (Genesis 5:3). In other words they inherited their father's spiritual nature as well as his physical nature, *and so do we.* This is what the theologians mean by 'original sin'. Man is born guilty and corrupt: as Paul puts it 'through the disobedience of the one man many were made sinners' (Romans 5:19). Perhaps nothing in the whole Bible more vividly describes the hopelessness of man's position if left to himself. He is literally *a born loser,* because he inherits from all his predecessors a guilty, fallen nature, and a fatal tendency to break God's law.

## And now the good news

As we have now seen, every sinner (in other words, every man) is guilty of breaking God's law, regardless of whether he knows or admits it. Then it also follows that every man deserves condemnation and punishment. What is more, the Bible repeatedly says that the punishment for sin is both physical and spiritual death (that is to say, eternal separation from God). In the book of Proverbs we are told 'he who pursues evil goes to his death' (Proverbs 11:19); God told Ezekiel 'the soul who sins is the one who will die' (Ezekiel 18:4); Paul says that 'the wages of sin is death' (Romans 6:23) and James says that 'sin when it is full-grown, gives birth to death' (James 1:15). The seriousness of sin can be judged by its result, which is to sever the link between man and his Maker.

Yet the amazing news contained in the Bible is that while every sinner deserves both condemnation and punishment, *he can escape both!* The Bible's one great message is that it is just here, at the point of man's utter helplessness, that God intervened in the person of the Lord Jesus Christ. The Apostle Paul calls Jesus 'the last Adam' (1 Corinthians 15:45) and this is a wonderful title, because the Bible tells us that he is able to restore to man all that the first Adam lost when he fell into sin. Although Jesus was (and is) God, *he became man.* As John puts it 'The Word (another name for Jesus) became flesh and lived for a while among us'

(John 1:14). As a man, he was subject to all the spiritual pressures that face us today, yet in the face of them all he remained 'without sin' (Hebrews 4:15). Where Adam yielded, Jesus resisted; where Adam fell, Jesus stood; where Adam failed, Jesus conquered. But that was not all. Having resisted every attack of the devil, having refused to give way to any spiritual pressure, having never once sinned, he then agreed to be put to death, and to take the place of guilty sinners by bearing in his own body God's righteous judgment against human sin. And he did all of this so that people like you and me could be released from the condemnation and punishment that our sin deserves, and brought into a right relationship with God. In Paul's tremendous words, 'God made him who had no sin to be sin for us, so that in him we might become the righteousness of God' (2 Corinthians 5:21).

But that is still not the end of the story. Jesus not only bore the punishment for men's sins in his death on the cross, He rose again from the dead and is able to give men power to conquer sin in their daily lives. As Paul puts it, 'I can do everything through him who gives me strength' (Philippians 4:13). No wonder what God did in sending Jesus into the world is called 'the gospel', or good news! The guilty sinner can be declared righteous; the condemned man can be set free; the man who was biased from birth can become holy; the man destined for hell can reach heaven. But how? That is what we shall look at in the next three chapters.

# Two — How can I find God?

---

## 3. NEW BIRTH

The Bible is the Word of God, and the final written authority in all matters of Christian faith and practice. It contains everything that a man needs to know in order to find God. But the way to God is not set out like a mathematical equation. The Bible is a collection of 66 books written by about 40 authors over a period of some 1,500 years, and contains history, poetry, prophecy and many other ways of expressing the truth. It also contains no fewer than 1,189 chapters. So where does a man start in trying to find his way to God?

### Entrance this way only

In the Bible, becoming a Christian is described as becoming a member of the Kingdom of Heaven, or the Kingdom of God, and there are two sayings of Jesus that crystallise exactly what a man needs in order for this great change to come about in his life. In the first he tells an influential religious leader called Nicodemus 'Unless a man is born again, he cannot see the Kingdom of God' (John 3:3). In the second he tells his disciples 'Unless you change and become like little children, you will never enter the kingdom of heaven' (Matthew 18:3). There you have it in a nutshell. If a man is going to become a Christian, two things are necessary: he must be 'born again' and he must be 'changed' (or as we sometimes say 'converted'). We are going to study these two expressions in three chapters in order to answer the question 'How can I find God?' In this chapter, we shall look at what it means to be 'born again'.

## Back to the bad news

It is interesting to notice that it was to a very religious person that Jesus spoke about the need of the new birth, and it is often such people who refuse to accept that such a change is necessary. They say: 'I live a decent kind of life. I show love to others. I try to be kind and unselfish. I go to church. I read my Bible. I say my prayers. I have been baptised. Why all this business about needing to be born again?' But that person has forgotten (or never realised) the bad news we studied earlier, which is that left to himself, man is *'dead* in . . . transgressions and sins' (Ephesians 2:1). Paul tells the Colossians that before they became Christians they were *'dead* in your sins' (Colossians 2:13), and Jesus describes a Christian as someone who has 'crossed over from *death* unto life' (John 5:24).

In each case, the Bible is speaking about *spiritual* death, which is very different from physical death. Physical death is like the end of a journey, when one passes from time into eternity. Spiritual death is separation from God, while final, eternal separation from God is what the Bible calls hell or 'the second death' (Revelation 20:14); and because man is by nature and practice spiritually dead he needs to receive spiritual life, in other words, to be 'born again'.

We can illustrate man's spiritual need in other ways. For instance, dead men are blind; and Jesus said that unless a man is born again 'he cannot *see* the kingdom of God', while Paul adds that 'the god of this age (the devil) has blinded the minds of unbelievers, so that they cannot see the light of the gospel of the glory of Christ, who is the image of God' (2 Corinthians 4:4). Again, dead men are deaf; and the prophet Jeremiah says of people who are not right with God 'Their ears are closed so they cannot hear' (Jeremiah 6:10). Speaking of spiritual things to someone who has never been born again is like showing a Rembrandt to a blind man, or asking a person who is stone deaf for his verdict on a Beethoven sonata.

Or to take one more illustration, a dead body soon becomes decayed and unclean; and the Bible repeatedly teaches that even at our best we are unclean in God's sight until we are born again. An Old Testament writer asks 'Who can say, "I have kept my heart pure; I am clean and without sin"?' (Proverbs 20:9), and the last book in the Bible says concerning heaven that 'nothing impure will ever enter it, nor will anyone who does what is shameful or deceitful' (Revelation 21:27). If those were the only two verses in the Bible, it would be obvious that for a man to get right with God something radical needs to happen to him.

But what about those good works, religious ceremonies, respectability, sincerity and all the other things on which so many people pin their hopes of heaven? They are no more effective in producing life than wreaths on a coffin, or decorations on a corpse! In fact, even the character of the best things we do or say is polluted in the sight of God, for the Bible says bluntly that 'all of us have become like one who is unclean, and all our righteous acts are like filthy rags' (Isaiah 64:6).

### God is not man

A second reason why we need to be born again is that

to get right with God is not to strike a bargain with an equal, but to enter into a new relationship with someone who is altogether different in nature. In the Old Testament, Ezra says 'O Lord, God of Israel, you are righteous! . . . Here we are before you in our guilt' (Ezra 9:15) and the prophet Habakkuk says of God 'Your eyes are too pure to look on evil' (Habakkuk 1:13). Turning to the New Testament, we discover Jesus saying 'Blessed are the pure in heart, for they will see God' (Matthew 5:8). God and man are so different in essence, in character and in nature, that the only way in which man can possibly enter into a living relationship with him is if God gives him a new life, a new nature. As Jesus told Nicodemus 'Flesh gives birth to flesh, but the Spirit gives birth to spirit. You should not be surprised at my saying "You must be born again".' (John 3:6–7).

## Beware of imitations

Advertisers of quality products sometimes use this expression to warn people about settling for something less than 'the real thing', and it is certainly a necessary warning in the spiritual world. For instance, the new birth is not just a greater understanding of biblical truth, a kind of theological wash and brush up. It is possible to know the Bible from beginning to end and to remain spiritually dead and unmoved. Neither is the new birth just a matter of moral improvement. That is reformation; the new birth is regeneration. It is not just a matter of turning over a new leaf, but of receiving a new life. Neither is the new birth just a psychological experience, some kind of natural religious crisis. Hardly anything could be further from the truth. The new birth is a supernatural work of God in the heart of man, a miracle which can neither be explained nor controlled. In the words of Jesus 'The wind blows wherever it pleases. You may hear its sound, but you cannot tell where it comes from or where it is going. So it is with everyone born of the spirit' (John 3:8). Beware of imitations! A Christian is a person who has experienced a spiritual re-birth '. . . not of natural descent, nor of human decision or a husband's will, *but born of God'* (John 1:13). Has God worked that miracle in your own heart and life? Are you *sure?* As we shall see later, there are certain results that always follow the new birth, and which help to confirm that the miracle has taken place, but if you have any doubt in your own mind as to whether you have ever been born again, then turn to God in prayer *now,* confess your sin, tell him of your need, and ask him to have mercy on you, and to give you this priceless gift.

## New birth: New life

Natural life involves relationships and responsibilities — and so does spiritual life. When you become a Christian, you are immediately related to God as a son or daughter, (and, incidentally, to every other Christian in heaven and on earth as a brother or sister). But relationship brings responsibility, and the privilege of new birth brings with it not only all the potential of a new life, but also the greatest responsibilities that any man could ever have. In natural birth, a child receives a life to be lived, a nature to be developed, and powers to be used, and each of these can be used as a picture of what we receive when we are born again.

### *Firstly, the gift of a new life to be lived for God*

Have you ever noticed how excited the Apostle John gets about being a Christian? — 'How great is the love the Father has lavished on us, that we should be called children of God! And that is what we are!' (1 John 3:1). The more we learn of God's great love for us in Christ, the more marvellous it will be to us that he should have drawn us into his family. But remember, privilege brings responsibility! This is how Paul puts it — '(Christ) died for all that those who live should no longer live for themselves, but for him who died for them and was raised again' (2 Corinthians 5:15). There is the perfect slogan for Christians! Their lives should be lived *'no longer . . . for themselves, but for him'*. Just as human parents look keenly at the life of the developing child to see if it bears any likeness to father or mother, so God looks at the Christian longing that the character and conduct of Jesus should become increasingly obvious. Are you a Christian? Then let me ask you this question: are you becoming steadily more like Jesus? If you are not, then you are a disappointment to your heavenly Father, because the Bible tells us clearly that Christians are 'predestined to be conformed to the likeness of (God's) Son' (Romans 8:29).

*Secondly, the gift of a new nature to be developed for God*

One of the most astonishing things the Bible says about becoming a Christian is that 'we participate in the divine nature' (2 Peter 1:4). God comes to dwell within us in the Person of the Holy Spirit and, if I can put it in this way, he brings his own likes and dislikes, his own divine appreciation and understanding of right and wrong. The result is revolutionary! Notice how Paul describes the way in which his readers at Ephesus used to behave before they became Christians. He speaks of the way 'in which you used to live when you followed the ways of this world and of the ruler of the kingdom of the air, the spirit who is now at work in those who are disobedient. All of us also lived among them at one time, gratifying the cravings of our sinful nature and following its desires and thoughts. Like the rest, we were by nature objects of wrath' (Ephesians 2:2—3). In their unconverted days they were carried along by the desires and thoughts of their sinful, corrupt natures. But the Christian finds himself in a different position. He finds himself indwelt by the very nature of God; he finds himself saying with David 'To do your will, O my God, is my desire; your law is within my heart' (Psalm 40:8). The old nature is not removed, but it no longer has control. Instead of spineless consent, the Christian finds that temptation brings spiritual conflict. As Paul puts it, 'So I say, live by the Spirit, and you will not gratify the desires of the sinful nature. For the sinful nature desires what is contrary to the Spirit, and the Spirit what is contrary to the sinful nature. They are in conflict with each other, so that you do not do what you want' (Galatians 5:16—17). As a Christian you should never cease praying that this new divine nature will assert a growing ascendancy over your mind, heart, will, spirit, and conscience, and you should learn to do so in the assurance that 'it is God who works in you to will and to act according to his good purpose' (Philippians 2:13).

*Thirdly, the gift of new powers to be used for God*
Just as the new-born child has physical powers to be used, so the new-born child of God has spiritual powers to be used. Peter says 'Grace and peace be yours in abundance through the knowledge of God and of Jesus our Lord. His divine power has given us everything we need for life and godliness through our knowledge of

him who called us by his own glory and goodness. Through these he has given us his very great and precious promises, so that through them you may participate in the divine nature and escape the corruption in the world caused by evil desires' (2 Peter 1:2–4). Just as every new-born child has tremendous potential in that tiny body, so the child of God has fantastic spiritual potential for Christian influence and service. Every man has been given talents, gifts and abilities; every Christian has a special, enlightened responsibility to use those gifts for the glory of God and the blessing of others.

In the living of his new life, in the development of his new nature, and in the use of his new powers, the Christian has a constant responsibility to demonstrate the reality of his spiritual birth by the quality of his spiritual life. We shall look at this side of things in the second part of the book – the section called 'Living the Christian Life'. Meantime, we need to go back to the other essential factors in becoming a Christian.

## 4. REPENTANCE

In the last chapter we looked at the first of two statements Jesus made to indicate the only way in which a person can get right with God – 'Unless a man is born again he cannot see the kingdom of God' (John 3:3). In this chapter and the one which follows we shall examine the second statement – 'Unless you change and become like little children, you will never enter the kingdom of heaven' (Matthew 18:3). This 'change' is commonly called 'conversion' and we shall look at it in two separate chapters. This is because conversion has two distinct elements, repentance and faith, and it will be helpful to look at each of them separately.

**No laughing matter**

To the average man in the street, the word 'repent' is a kind of religious joke word. It is part of the cartoonist's stock in trade; when he wants to depict a narrow-minded religious fanatic, he draws a man holding a sandwich board with the words 'Repent, sinner, repent!' plastered across it. But you only have to read the Bible with an open mind to see that far from being something casual, or even symbolic, repentance is one of the most important subjects to which a man could ever give attention. God warns the people of Israel 'Repent! Turn from your idols' (Ezekiel 14:6). Later on he commands them 'Repent! Turn away from all your offences' (Ezekiel 18:30). The heart of John the Baptist's message was 'Repent, for the kingdom of heaven is near' (Matthew 3:2). Jesus began his public ministry with the same words, 'Repent, for the kingdom of heaven is near' (Matthew 4:17). When the inner circle of twelve disciples began their preaching, we read that 'they went out and preached that people should repent' (Mark 6:12). When the crowds listening to the Apostle Peter on the Day of Pentecost were shattered by his preaching, and asked what they should do, his reply was 'Repent, and be baptised every one of you, in the name of Jesus Christ so that your sins may be forgiven' (Acts 2:38). In the course of his great sermon at Athens, Paul told his hearers that God 'commands all people everywhere to repent' (Acts 17:30). With that kind of evidence in front of us, we cannot afford to treat repentance as a laughing matter. What man thinks funny, God puts first. It is serious, vital, essential, and urgent.

**What does it mean?**

Repentance is certainly a much misunderstood word,

and most people's view of it is inadequate. Some think it merely means acknowledging one's sin; others think it means being sorry; but it means much more.

## *Repentance involves knowledge*

Jesus once told a story which began like this — 'What do you think? There was a man who had two sons. He went to the first and said "Son, go and work today in the vineyard." "I will not", he answered, but later he changed his mind and went'. (Matthew 21:28—29). Here is a clear picture of what repentance means. The son's first reaction to his father's order was to say 'Nothing doing', but after thinking it over he changed his mind, and did what he was told. He recognised his father's right to command and his own duty to obey. And that is exactly where repentance begins. To repent is to change your mind about God, about Jesus, about sin and about yourself. It is to recognise that you are a sinner, and that as the sovereign Lord of the universe, God has the right to control and direct your life.

## Repentance involves feelings

A few hours before Jesus was arrested, Peter promised him that he would never deny or disown him 'even if all fall away on account of you' (Matthew 26:33). But when the heat was turned on he soon found himself cornered, and three times he denied that he even knew Jesus. The Bible then tells us that 'Immediately a cock crowed. Then Peter remembered the word Jesus had spoken: "Before the cock crows, you will disown me three times" and he went outside and wept bitterly' (Matthew 26:74—75). Peter did not just come to a cold, analytical knowledge that he had sinned. His emotions were stirred by a solemn realisation of what he had done. He was ashamed and broken-hearted that he could have done such a thing. Repentance involves sorrow for sin.

## Repentance involves determination

The story of the Prodigal Son gives a good illustration of this. After he had left home, gone his own way, squandered his fortune, and been reduced to eating pig-swill, we read that he said 'I will set out and go back to my father' (Luke 15:18). He not only realised what he had done, and regretted it deeply, he determined to do something about it. He made up his mind that he would go back home and cast himself on his father's mercy, turning his back on the life-style that had ruined him. Repentance involves determination to change — but even that is not enough.

## Repentance involves action

True repentance not only clears a man's head, moves his heart and nerves his will — it gets into his feet! The prodigal son's repentance is not proved to be real until we read the words 'So he got up and went to his father' (Luke 15:20). Repentance is the first step a man takes on his way back to God, and without it anything else he might do leaves him lost. Repentance is not merely knowing about your sin, weeping over it, and determining to do something about it. It also means turning your back on it and heading towards God. Have you done that? It is not difficult to check on this, because true repentance produces a changed life. When a crowd of Pharisees and Sadducees, some of the bitterest opponents Jesus ever faced, came to John the Baptist and asked for baptism, he turned them down flat with the words 'Produce fruit in keeping with repentance' (Matthew 3:8). Only when their lives had changed would he accept that they had truly repented. Repentance without moral change is a contradiction in terms.

## God has ways and means

When a group of Christians get together and discuss the ways in which they were brought to a living experience of God, it is fascinating to discover the many different means that were used to bring about their conversion. Both in the Bible and by the testimonies of God's people down the ages, we discover that repentance is produced by many different means.

### *Primarily through the preaching of the gospel*

Jesus once told the scribes and Pharisees 'The men of Nineveh will stand up at the judgment with this generation and condemn it; for they repented at the preaching of Jonah, and now one greater than Jonah is here' (Matthew 12:41). Although disobedient at first, Jonah eventually obeyed God's instructions to preach a stern message of warning to the people of Nineveh, as a result of which 'the Ninevites believed God. They declared a fast, and all of them, from the greatest to the least, put on sackcloth' (Jonah 3:5). The impact of Jonah's preaching drove them to repentance, faith — and salvation! You have the same picture in the New Testament. On the Day of Pentecost 3,000 people were converted as the result of Peter's preaching. Reminding the Thessalonians of their Christian beginnings, Paul tells them that he and his colleagues had 'preached the gospel of God to you' (1 Thessalonians 2:9). Someone has said that we live today in an age of discussion-circle Christianity. It is no longer thought right to be dogmatic. Every argument must be open-ended. One man's opinion is as good as the next. Vagueness is the vogue. The sharp-edged blacks and whites must merge together and become comfortable and undemanding greys. But that is not what we find in the Bible, where the striaghtforward, uncompromising declaration of the truth is given an indispensable place. After assuring his readers that 'Everyone who calls on the name of the Lord will be saved' (Romans 10:13), Paul goes on to ask 'How, then, can they call on the one they have not believed in? And how can they believe in the one of whom they have not heard? And how can they hear without someone preaching to them?' (Romans 10:14). In formal preaching, writing, broadcasting, and conversation, God continues to use the straightforward assertion of biblical truth, and through the application of that truth to men's hearts produces repentance and faith.

### Sometimes through sorrow

Recounting the experiences of the people of Israel, the Psalmist says 'Whenever God slew them, they would seek him; they eagerly turned to him again' (Psalm 78:34). The writer of another Psalm gives his own testimony — 'Before I was afflicted I went astray, but now I obey your word' (Psalm 119:67). It was when trouble was falling about his ears thick and fast that Pharaoh finally broke down and cried 'This time I have sinned. The Lord is in the right, and I and my people are in the wrong' (Exodus 9:27). So today, many people are brought to a sense of sin, and an experience of repentance, through trial, stress, pressure, sorrow, sickness or bereavement. Men can sometimes see farther through a tear than through a telescope!

### Sometimes through joy

Paul challenges the Romans 'Do you show contempt

for the riches of (God's) kindness, tolerance and patience, not realising that God's kindness leads you towards repentance?' (Romans 2:4). Writing about the promise of Christ's return to the earth, and of the sceptics who said it would never happen, Peter says, 'The Lord is not slow in keeping his promise, as some understand slowness. He is patient with you, not wanting anyone to perish, but everyone to come to repentance' (2 Peter 3:9). Many a person has been led to repentance, not through some harrowing experience, but through exactly the reverse – a tremendous sense of the goodness of God in providing all his needs, and in giving him so many things that bring joy into his life.

## Sometimes through emptiness

One of the wisest men in the Old Testament, after trying to live it up in every imaginable way, wrote 'Yet when I surveyed all that my hands had done and what I had toiled to achieve, everything was meaningless, a chasing after the wind; nothing was gained under the sun' (Ecclesiastes 2:11). It is a simple fact that none of the things men chase after in order to find fulfilment in life – wealth, popularity, sex, music, success in business, sport, drugs, travel, health or material possessions – can ever bring ultimate satisfaction to the human spirit. Man was made for God, and until he finds him there will always be a basic emptiness in life. It is often a sense of this basic emptiness, a feeling of failure, frustration and disappointment, that begins to turn men's thoughts towards God, and eventually leads them to repentance.

Yet the means are not as important as the fact, and before we go any further, let me again ask you the all-important question: have you experienced true repentance? Have you changed your mind, your heart, your will? Have you changed the direction of your life? Without genuine repentance, there is no way back to God. As Jesus said so plainly, 'unless you repent, you too will all perish' (Luke 13:5).

## 5. FAITH

If the word 'repentance' is misunderstood, then the word 'faith' is even more so. To many people, it all seems so unreal, intangible, 'airy-fairy'. Perhaps more people than we imagine would agree with the schoolboy's definition of faith as 'believing that a thing is true when all the time you know is isn't'! But that is very different from the Bible's definition of the word. This is what we read in the Epistle to the Hebrews — 'Now faith is being sure of what we hope for and certain of what we do not see' (Hebrews 11:1). In other words, biblical faith is not 'Believe it and it will be true', but 'It *is* true, believe it'!

### Faith is a fact

Perhaps part of men's difficulty about the word 'faith' is because it is usually thought of as a religious thing. Yet faith is something we use every day, in all kinds of circumstances.

### *In the scientific laboratory*

An eminent American scientist has said that basically, scientists live by faith. They perform many experiments by faith. They accept information by faith. No scientist has ever seen an electron or proton, yet there is no scientist who does not believe in these atomic particles. Again, the scientist pins his faith on what the textbooks tell him is truth, even though we know that those same textbooks are being constantly modified, revised and changed to keep pace with each new discovery.

### At the meal-table

Travelling through a strange town, you walk into a restaurant, call for a menu, and order a meal. When it is served, you eat it without question, and in doing so you exercise all three aspects of faith — knowledge, belief and trust. You *know* that a restaurant serves food, you *believe* that they will take your order, and you *trust* everyone involved in producing the food on your plate.

### Walking along the road

You come to crossroads. The traffic lights on the road you want to cross turn red. You *know* that that means the traffic on that road must stop, you *believe* that it will, and you *trust* the drivers concerned by walking across the road in front of their vehicles. Here again are the three elements in faith.

### At the bank

Wanting to put some money away for a rainy day, and to invest it wisely, you decide to open a Deposit Account at your bank. You *know* that banks do this sort of thing, you *believe* that your local bank can be relied upon to do its job effectively, and you hand your money across the counter without hesitation, *trusting* the bank to do all it promises to do.

### Getting married

Boy meets girl. Friendship ripens into love. Finally, the great day dawns, and they stand together before God and man and pledge themselves to each other. And that wedding ceremony is the climax of their growing and mutual faith. First, they got to *know* each other, then to *believe* in each other, and finally to *trust* or commit themselves to each other in holy matrimony.

So we could go on, adding to the day by day examples of the way in which we exercise faith. Yet no human example of faith is quite perfect. The scientific experiment might fail, the food might be 'off', a car driver might jump the lights and knock you down, the bank might collapse, one of the partners to a marriage might break those solemn vows. But when we put our faith in God, no such failure is possible, for the Bible says that 'God . . . does not lie' (Titus 1:2) and that 'He who promised is faithful' (Hebrews 10:23).

### Back to the Bible

In the New Testament, there are many incidents which vividly illustrate the nature of faith. Let us focus on just one of them, told in Mark 5. The story centres around a woman who had been suffering from some kind of haemorrhage for twelve years, and was apparently incurable. This is how the story goes on — 'When she heard about Jesus, she came up behind him in the crowd and touched his cloak, because she thought, "If I just touch his clothes, I will be healed". Immediately her bleeding stopped and she felt in her body that she was freed from her suffering. At once Jesus realised that power had gone out from him. He turned around in the crowd and asked, "Who touched my clothes?" "You see the people crowding against you," his disciples answered, "and yet you can ask, 'Who touched me?' " But Jesus kept looking around to see who had done it. Then the woman, knowing what had happened to her, came and fell at his feet and, trembling with fear, told him the whole truth. He said to her, "Daughter, your faith has healed you. Go in peace, and be freed from your suffering" ' (Mark 5:27–34).

Notice that here again we have the three elements involved in faith. Firstly, there was *knowledge* – 'she heard about Jesus'. Perhaps she had heard him preach; certainly she had heard other people speak of the wonderful person he was, and of the extraordinary miracles he had performed. Secondly, there was *belief* – she thought to herself 'If I just touch his clothes, I will be healed'. This was no shot in the dark, or clutching at straws; she was absolutely convinced that this man who had healed so many others would heal her if she could only so much as touch the clothes he was wearing. Thirdly, there was *trust* – she 'touched his cloak'. And what happened? 'Immediately her bleeding stopped, and she felt in her body that she was freed from her bleeding'.

The whole story can be used as an illustration of the way in which a sinner comes to Christ for salvation. He must *know* about him, he must *believe* that he is willing and able to save him, and he must *trust* him to do so. Have you ever exercised faith in the Lord Jesus Christ in that way? It is not enough to know the facts about his birth, life, death and resurrection. Nor is it enough to believe that, as the Bible says, 'Christ Jesus came into the world to save sinners' (1 Timothy 1:15). A person does not become a Christian by accepting certain historical facts, nor by believing in a theological statement. *Saving faith is not consent to a proposition, but commitment to a person,* and that person is the Lord Jesus Christ, the Son of God and the Saviour of men. Before going on to the next section of the book, make quite sure that that is what you have done; that, having repented and turned from your sin, you have put your trust in the Lord Jesus Christ.

The Apostle Paul told the church at Ephesus that the whole thrust of his preaching was to urge his hearers to 'turn to God in repentance and have faith in our Lord Jesus' (Acts 20:21).

There is no other way of becoming a Christian.

# Three — What does God offer me?

## 6. JUSTIFICATION

The word 'justification' is one of the longest words in the New Testament — and one of the greatest and most important words in Christian doctrine. Many Christians I know have lived for years with an inadequate view of what it is to be a Christian because of their failure to understand what this marvellous word involves. That being so, the time you spend reading (and if necessary, re-reading) this chapter will be well spent.

### Window on the word

In reading the Bible, you will often find that a word used in the New Testament is illustrated by a passage in the Old Testament, giving us a 'window' into the meaning of the word concerned. Here, for instance, is a good example of the meaning of the word 'justification'. Included in the laws for the government of the people of Israel was this one — 'When men have a dispute, they are to take it to court and the judges will decide the case, acquitting the innocent and condemning the guilty'. (Deuteronomy 25:1). The picture is clear: if, after hearing the evidence, the judge decided that a man was not guilty of the offence alleged against him, then he should be *declared 'not guilty'* — and that is the precise meaning of the word 'justified'. Justification is an act that puts a man right as to his standing or position in a court of law, and it is an act that can only be performed by the judge in that court. It would obviously be wrong for a judge to declare a man innocent if he knew him to be guilty, or guilty if he knew him to be innocent, and the Bible underlines this very plainly – 'Acquitting the guilty and condemning the innocent – the Lord detests them both' (Proverbs 17:15). But if that were all that the Bible had to say on the subject, 'justification' would be the darkest word in the English language, because, as we have already seen, we are all guilty before God, and condemned by nature and practice. If only innocent men can be acquitted, not one person in the world will ever get to heaven.

### The 'impossible' truth

It is exactly at this point that we come across one of the most amazing truths in the whole Bible. This is how Paul puts it in two places in his Epistle to the Romans – Firstly he says, 'Now when a man works, his wages are not credited to him as a gift, but as an obligation. However, to the man who does not work but trusts God who justifies the wicked, his faith is credited as righteousness' (Romans 4:4–5). Secondly (though in fact a little earlier in the Epistle) he speaks of Christians as being 'justified freely by (God's) grace through the redemption that came by Christ Jesus. God presented him as a sacrifice of atonement, through faith in his blood. He did this to demonstrate his justice, because in his forbearance he had left the sins committed beforehand unpunished – he did it to demonstrate his justice at the present time, so as to be just and the one who justifies the man who has faith in Jesus' (Romans 3:24–26).

Those are two of the most staggering statements in

the whole Bible. They say that God actually justifies guilty sinners (that is to say, declares them to be holy in his sight), that he does so because of what Jesus accomplished through his death on the cross, and that he grants this justification not as the result of a man's efforts at good living, but purely as a free gift, to be received by faith. It is almost too good to be true! Let us look at it more closely.

## The substitute

Faced with Paul's statement that God 'justifies the wicked', the obvious question to ask is 'But how can he possibly do that when, by his own law, the guilty man should be punished, and only the innocent acquitted?' The Bible's answer is that in Jesus Christ, God provided *a substitute for the sinner*. When Jesus came to the earth, was born as a human being, lived a perfect life, died, and rose again from the dead, he was doing so *on behalf of others*. To focus on the central issue here, the Bible says that when he died on the cross, Jesus was taking the place of others, bearing their sin, enduring their suffering, accepting their punishment, paying their penalty. The New Testament is absolutely clear on this. Jesus said 'This is my blood of the covenant, which is poured out for many for the forgiveness of sins' (Matthew 26:28). Paul says 'Christ died for the ungodly' (Romans 5:6); 'Christ died for us' (Romans 5:8); 'the Son of God . . . loved me and gave himself for me' (Galatians 2:20). Peter says 'For Christ died for sins once for all, the righteous for the unrighteous, to bring you to God' (1 Peter 3:18), and that 'He himself bore our sins in his body on the tree' (1 Peter 2:24). John says 'Jesus Christ laid down his life for us' (1 John 3:16).

In another stupendous statement on the subject,

Paul says 'God made him who had no sin to be sin for us, so that in him we might become the righteousness of God' (2 Corinthians 5:21). When we say that God justifies a man, we do not mean that he pronounces a guilty man to be innocent (which would be untrue), but that he is willing to accept the sacrifice of Christ on his behalf, and to pardon him on the basis of Christ's perfect life and substitutionary death.

## Free, gratis and for nothing

The next amazing thing we discover about justification is that because it cost Jesus everything, it costs man nothing! The *basis* of justification is the person and work of Christ; the *means* of justification (the way in which a man receives it) is by faith, and by faith alone. Notice how Paul insists on this. In one of the two key statements we have already looked at, he says that Christians are 'justified freely by (God's) grace' (Romans 3:24). Elsewhere, he says 'Therefore, the promise comes by faith, so that it may be by grace' (Romans 4:16). Putting it the other way around, he says 'For we maintain that a man is justified by faith apart from observing the law' (Romans 3:28), and again 'For it is by grace you have been saved, through faith — and this not from yourselves, it is the gift of God — not by works, so that no one can boast' (Ephesians 2:8—9). What an amazing thing! — yet millions of religious people have missed the whole, wonderful truth of what the Bible is saying at this point. Often with great sincerity, they are trying to 'earn' their justification. As Paul said of the Jews of his day, 'Since they did not know the righteousness that comes from God and sought to establish their own, they did not submit to God's righteousness. Christ is the end of the law so that there may be righteousness for everyone who believes' (Romans 10:3–4). There is no such thing as salvation by character; what men need is salvation *from* character! And God promises that salvation only to those who abandon trusting in their own efforts, or sincerity, or religion, or goodness, or anything else, and who cast themselves without reserve on the Lord Jesus Christ.

### Eyes open, mouth shut

'But', somebody asks, 'if I cannot be justified by my efforts to keep God's law, what is the purpose of the law? The Bible's answer to that question is that first of all 'through the law we become conscious of sin' (Romans 3:20). Even if the only 'law' part of the Bible was the passage we know as the Ten Commandments, that would be enough to show me that I am a sinner, someone who has broken God's law. Secondly, the Bible says that 'whatever the law says, it says to those who are under the law, so that every mouth may be stopped and the whole world held accountable to God' (Romans 3:19). Not only does God's law open my eyes to my guilt, it shuts my mouth when I try to excuse myself! And when the law brings me there, so that I turn away from trusting in myself to put my trust in Christ, it is doing exactly what it was intended to do. As Paul puts it, 'the Scripture declares that the whole world is a prisoner of sin, so that what was promised, being given through faith in Jesus Christ, might be given to those who believe. Before this faith came, we were held prisoners by the law, locked up until faith should be revealed. So the law was put in charge *to lead us to Christ* that we might be justified by faith' (Galatians 3:22–24).

God's law is still the perfect moral standard for the Christian life – but nobody becomes a Christian by his own efforts at keeping it.

## A miracle in 3-D

In trying to gather together some of the things we have discovered about justification, we could say that the Bible speaks of it in three dimensions. The Christian is said to be 'justified . . . by (God's) grace' (Romans 3:24); 'justified by (Christ's) blood' (Romans 5:9); and 'justified by faith' (Romans 3:28). A simple illustration will help to show how all three are true. We visit three homes in Manchester, asking the owners where their water supply comes from. The first man tells us that the water in his house comes from Thirlmere in the Lake District; the second tells us that it comes from the water pipes; the third says that it comes from the tap. Who is telling the truth? All three are! Lake Thirlmere is the source of the water, the pipes bring it into the house, and it is when the tap is turned on that the water flows. So the blood of Christ (in other words, the death of Christ) is the basis of justification; the grace of God brings it within reach of every man — Paul speaks of 'the grace of God that brings salvation' (Titus 2:11); and faith is the 'tap', the condition upon which the miracle of justification becomes real to a person.

## Negatives and positives

Now let us try very briefly to sum up the benefits that justification brings to a person. These are both negative and positive.

*Negatively,* justification removes the guilt of sin. God reckons the Christian as 'Not Guilty', because he sees him as being 'in Christ' (2 Corinthians 5:17). The perfect righteousness of Christ is the basis of God's judgment.

Justification also removes the penalty for sin, which is spiritual death. As Paul puts it, 'Therefore, there is now no condemnation for those who are in Christ Jesus' (Romans 8:1). God accepts the death of Christ as the full and complete payment of every penalty that his holy law requires. The death of Christ assures the full and free pardon of all of a Christian's sins, *past, present and future*. This does not mean that a Christian is perfect, and does not need daily forgiveness and cleansing — but we shall look at this in a later chapter. The all-important thing to realise at the moment is that justification is full, perfect, complete and final, and that it brings a person into a position from which he can never be removed.

*Positively,* justification brings to a person all the benefits of being a Christian — and the Bible is full of them. Whereas to be pardoned by an earthly judge would not bring any rewards, but only get rid of the past, justification brings with it a multitude of positive benefits. The Christian is not only spared the punishment for his sins, he is treated as if he had always been perfectly holy. When Satan tried to accuse Joshua, the high priest, in God's presence, we read that the angel told God's servant 'See I have taken away your sin, and I will put rich garments on you' (Zechariah 3:4). When the prodigal son returned home, his father said to his servants 'Quick! bring the best robe, and put it on him. Put a ring on his finger and sandals on his feet. Bring the fattened calf and kill it. Let's have a feast and celebrate' (Luke 15:22—23). And when a person becomes a Christian, God not only forgives the past, he pours out his blessing for the present and the future. The Christian is not only pardoned, he is promoted! We could sum up the positive benefits of justification by saying that the Christian receives two things. The first is *reconciliation:* Paul puts it like this — 'Therefore, since we have been justified through faith, we have peace with God through our Lord Jesus Christ'

(Romans 5:1). Once in rebellion against him, the Christian now stands in a totally different relationship to God. Unbelievers are God's enemies; Christians are his friends. The death of Christ has put away the one thing — sin — that kept them apart. But there is a second way of expressing this wonderful restoration of favour, and that is by saying that a Christian is *adopted* into God's family. This doctrine of adoption is so important and so full of meaning that we will look at it separately in the next chapter.

## A final picture

I hope that this chapter has been a help to you in understanding the wonderful biblical truths about justification. To help you to see the general outline again as simply as possible, here is a story that puts it in a nutshell. Two boys attend the same school. One works hard, goes on to further education, and eventually enters the legal profession. The other boy is a waster, drifts into bad company, and eventually falls foul of the law. Standing in the dock, he recognises the judge as his old school friend, and hopes that he might get off lightly under the 'Old Pals Act'! But when the sentence is passed it turns out to be the maximum — let us say £100 or six months' imprisonment. Given a final opportunity to say something, the prisoner pleads his old friendship with the judge and asks for leniency, but the judge explains that that would be impossible. With no money to pay the fine, the prisoner is led to the cells. Ten minutes later, the judge calls on him, and invites him out for a meal! The prisoner is bewildered. What about the sentence he must serve? How can he possibly walk out of the cell? The judge explains that someone has had pity on him and paid the £100 fine in full. As the demands of the law are now met in full, all he has to do is to accept the unknown friend's generosity and he is a free man. Later, over the meal, the ex-prisoner asks who could possibly have been so generous as to pay his fine. To his amazement, the judge explains that he himself had not only imposed the penalty, but had also paid it.

This is only a story — and it may never have happened in this or any other country — but it does help to illustrate what God, the judge of all the earth, has done for guilty sinners. God himself, in the person of the Lord Jesus Christ, paid sin's death penalty on the cross, and offers men a full and free pardon — justification — on the ground of Christ's sacrifice.

Of course, like all human stories, it falls short of the full wonder of what God has done, not least because when God justifies a sinner, he not only sets him free, he brings him into his own family. Christians receive what the Bible calls 'the full rights of sons' (Galatians 4:5) — and that is something altogether different!

## 7. ADOPTION

Of all the great words of Christianity, perhaps none has been so badly neglected as the one we are now going to study — 'adoption'. Yet it has a very important place in the vocabulary of the New Testament, and contains some marvellous truths for every Christian.

**When writing to Romans . . .**

In many countries today, adoption is a very common legal procedure, but it is interesting to notice the situation in the Middle East nearly 2,000 years ago, when the New Testament was written. Because of their own strict Old Testament laws relating to the passing on of property to their successors, the Jewish people had a very restricted law of adoption, and to many people it would be almost unknown. The Romans, on the other hand, had a detailed and complicated procedure built into their legal system. Under Roman law, a father had absolute rights over his son throughout his lifetime, which made his adoption into another family a very serious business, as it put him into the total possession and absolute control of another man. It also gave him a new name, a different legal standing, and all the rights of an heir in his new family.

With this background, it is fascinating to notice that there are five definitive references to adoption in the New Testament; three times in Paul's Epistle to the Romans, once when he was writing to the Galatians, and once in his letter to the Ephesians. Those who were at Rome would understand the picture of adoption, of course, but so would the readers of the other two letters, because Galatia was a Roman province, and Ephesus was the centre of Roman administration in that part of Asia. In other words, whenever Paul wrote of adoption, it was to people who would be able to use their knowledge of familiar legal and civil procedure to fill out its meaning. As today, society provided contemporary illustrations of what the Bible was saying!

### The Bible tells us so

When the Bible speaks of adoption in spiritual terms, what it means is that by an act of God, all those who are justified through faith in Christ are given the status of sons and daughters of God. They become members of his family, with all the rights and privileges involved. The new birth makes a person a child of God; adoption places a person in the position where he has the 'legal' rights of a son. In fact the very word 'adoption' literally means 'the placing of a son'. While spiritual adoption does not automatically change a person's character (any more than civil adoption) it does change his name, his standing, his rights, and above all, his relationship to God.

Perhaps it would help if we took a quick look at those five uses of the word 'adoption' in Paul's letters. Here they are in the order in which they appear:

'Because those who are led by the Spirit of God are sons of God. For you did not receive a spirit that makes you a slave again to fear, but you received the Spirit of sonship. And by him we cry, "*Abba*, Father." The Spirit himself testifies with our spirit that we are God's children. Now if we are children, then we are heirs — heirs of God and co-heirs with Christ, if indeed we share in his sufferings in order that we may also share in his glory' (Romans 8:14—17).

We know that the whole creation has been groaning as in the pains of childbirth right up to the present time. Not only so, but we ourselves, who have the firstfruits of the Spirit, groan inwardly as we wait eagerly for our adoption as sons, the redemption of our bodies' (Romans 8:22—23).

'. . . the people of Israel. Theirs is the adoption as sons; theirs the divine glory, the covenants, the receiving of the law, the temple worship and the promises' (Romans 9:4).

'But when the time had fully come, God sent his Son, born of a woman, born under law, to redeem those under law, that we might receive the full rights of sons. Because you are sons, God sent the Spirit of his Son into our hearts, the Spirit who calls out, "*Abba*, Father." So you are no longer a slave, but a son; and since you are a son, God has made you also an heir' (Galatians 4:4—7).

'For (God) chose us in (Christ) before the creation of the world to be holy and blameless in his sight. In love he predestined us to be adopted as his sons through Jesus Christ, in accordance with his pleasure and will – to the praise of his glorious grace, which he has freely given us in the One he loves' (Ephesians 1:4–6).

That, in a nutshell, is what the Bible tells us about spiritual adoption. Now we can look at some of this marvellous truth in more detail.

### From eternity to eternity

If you were to ask '*When* is a Christian adopted into God's family?', the correct answer would be 'He was in the past; he is at present; and he will be in the future' – because the Bible speaks of adoption in all three tenses.

#### The past tense

The quotation from Ephesians tells us that Christians were chosen in Christ before the foundation of the world and 'predestined . . . to be adopted as sons'. This marvellous truth is impossible to understand, but imperative to believe. What the theologians call the doctrine of election – the truth that from eternity God chose out a people for himself – runs throughout the whole Bible, and is specifically mentioned here with regard to adoption. A Christian is a member of God's family, with all the rights and privileges involved, not because he chose God as a father, but because God chose him as a son – and that choosing was done not only before the man concerned was born, but before even the world was made.

#### The present tense

Then there is a moment when what has always been

present in the mind and purpose of God becomes the personal experience of the person concerned, and that moment is when he turns from his sin and puts his trust in Jesus Christ as his own personal Saviour. The quotation from Galatians tells us that Jesus came into the world in order that believers might 'receive the full rights of sons', and in the first quotation from Romans 8 Paul reminds his hearers 'you have received the Spirit of sonship'. The moment of their conversion was the moment of their adoption.

### The future tense

Needless to say, the world does not recognise even the best Christians as children of God. But in the second of our quotations from Romans 8, Paul looks forward to 'the redemption of our bodies', the moment when the whole wonderful process of our adoption will be complete and the whole universe will see us to be truly the sons of God. The heir to the throne may go almost unnoticed in a family photograph of the Royal Family, but when the moment comes for him to be crowned, the whole world will recognise him: and John dares to say that when the great moment comes for Christ to return to the earth in power and glory, 'we shall be like him, for we shall see him as he is' (1 John 3:2). As Paul tells the Philippians, when the Lord Jesus Christ returns to earth he will (transform our lowly bodies so that they will be like his glorious body' (Philippians 3:21). There will be no doubt then that Christians have been adopted into God's eternal family! That will be the moment of truth. As Paul puts it 'The creation waits in eager expectation for the sons of God to be revealed' (Romans 8:19).

### The family heritage

As we saw earlier, a child adopted into a Roman family

entered immediately into all the rights and privileges of that family, just as if he had been born into it. In the same way, a Christian enters into sonship immediately on his conversion, and in so doing he receives a number of wonderful privileges.

## The Holy Spirit

We shall devote a separate chapter to the person and work of the Holy Spirit later, but at this point we just need to underline Paul's word to the Galatians — 'Because you are sons, God sent the Spirit of his Son (that is, the Holy Spirit) into our hearts'; and his word to the Romans — 'you received the Spirit of sonship (again, the Holy Spirit)'. As we shall see in the later chapter, this is absolutely fundamental to our understanding of the work of the Holy Spirit in the life of the Christian. Every Christian without exception has received the Holy Spirit. He not only performed the work of placing us in the family of God, he came and indwelt us at the moment of our conversion. The Bible is crystal clear about this — 'if anyone does not have the Spirit of Christ' (yet another title for the Holy Spirit) 'he does not belong to Christ' (Romans 8:9).

## A new relationship

It is interesting to notice that in our basic passages about adoption Paul mentions one specific result of the Holy Spirit's presence in the heart of the Christian. He tells the Romans that 'by him we cry, "*Abba, Father*" '; and he tells the Galatians 'God sent the Spirit of his Son into our hearts, the Spirit who calls out "*Abba*, Father".' The word '*Abba*' is not Greek, but Aramaic, a widely used language in the Middle East at that time. It was an intimate, familiar word that would be used by a child in speaking informally to its father. The only other time it is used in the New Testament is when Jesus, under tremendous pressure in the Garden of Gethsemane cries out '*Abba,* Father, everything is possible for you' (Mark 14:36). The relationship of the Christian to God the Father is such that he can call him by the same intimate name used by Jesus! Whenever you feel a warm, intimate fellowship with the Lord in prayer, and feel drawn to him as your heavenly Father, this is the work of the Holy Spirit confirming the deep sense in your own spirit that you are a child of God.

### A new name

Just as under Roman law a child took the name of his adopting father, so the Christian takes the name of his heavenly Father. Telling the Christians at Ephesus that he is aware of the pressures they are facing, Paul says 'For this reason I kneel before the Father, from whom his whole family of believers in heaven and on earth derives its name' (Ephesians 3:14—15); and he reminds the Galatians 'You are all sons of God through faith in Christ Jesus' (Galatians 3:26).

### A growing likeness

A little earlier, we saw that Christians were 'predestined . . . to be adopted as sons', but alongside that we need to put another tremendous truth, and that is that 'those God foreknew he also predestined to be conformed to the likeness of his Son' (Romans 8:29). We were not merely chosen to be saved, but to be holy, to become more and more like the Lord Jesus Christ in our daily lives. In human relationships, a father tries his hardest to mould the character of his adopted son along what he believes are the right lines. In Christian adoption, the presence of the Holy Spirit in the life of the believer *ensures* that there will be a growing family likeness. The Christian is not only commanded to 'grow in the grace and knowledge of our Lord and Saviour Jesus Christ' (2 Peter 3:18), *he is given the desire and the ability to do so.* As Paul wrote to the Philippians, 'it is God who works in you to will and to act according to his good purpose' (Philippians 2:13).

## All-round protection

Centuries before the Apostle Paul, the Psalmist wrote 'As the mountains surround Jerusalem, so the Lord surrounds his people, both now and for evermore' (Psalm 125:2). The Christian not only has the power of the Holy Spirit within him, but the protection of the Father round about him! The conscious presence of God, especially in the emergencies of life, is one of the great privileges enjoyed by his adopted sons and daughters.

## Necessary discipline

In words originally written to Jews who had become Christians, the Bible says 'you have forgotten that word of encouragement that addresses you as sons: "My son, do not make light of the Lord's discipline, and do not lose heart when he rebukes you, because the Lord disciplines those he loves, and he punishes everyone he accepts as a son". Endure hardship as discipline; God is treating you as sons. For what son is not disciplined by his father? If you are not disciplined (and everyone undergoes discipline), then you are illegitimate children and not true sons. Moreover, we have all had human fathers who disciplined us and we respected them for it. How much more should we submit to the Father of our spirits and live! Our fathers disciplined us for a little while as they thought best; but God disciplines us for our good, that we may share in his holiness' (Hebrews 12:5–10). That hardly needs any comment! The word 'discipline' means 'training', and when a father disciplines a child it is an act of love, an action deliberately calculated to be for the good of the child. It may be painful – to both father and child – but the end justifies the means. In the Christian life, God sometimes causes or allows his children to endure hardship or suffering, but it is always intended to result in his glory and their blessing. The more a Christian grows in grace, the more he will come to see that even the hard things in life are under God's control, and the more he will be willing to praise the Lord for the discipline that trains him towards Christian maturity, and prepares him for his ultimate goal.

### The riches of heaven

Perhaps the most staggering thing Paul says in the first quotation we looked at in his letter to the Romans is that 'we are God's children. Now if we are children, then we are heirs – heirs of God and co-heirs with Christ, if indeed we share in his sufferings in order that we may also share in his glory'. Just as certainly as Christians suffer rejection by the ungodly here on earth they will inherit all the riches of heaven in the world to come. They are 'fellow heirs with Christ', and Christ is the 'heir of all things' (Hebrews 1:2). Christians are called upon to bear a cross on earth, but they are also promised that they will wear a crown in heaven! As adopted sons of God, and fellow heirs with Christ, they will share in his glory for ever.

## 8. ASSURANCE

We come now to yet another key word in Christian vocabulary — 'assurance'. This is the biblical doctrine that a person who is born again, justified, and adopted (to use the phrases we studied in previous chapters) may *know* that he is a child of God, freed from the guilt and penalty of sin, and an inheritor of the kingdom of heaven.

### The man who knew

The doctrine of assurance runs like a golden thread throughout the Bible, but no book mentions it more often in proportion to its length than the First Epistle of John. In fact, he says that it was the importance of assurance that prompted the letter in the first place — 'I write these things to you who believe in the name of the Son of God, that you may *know* that you have eternal life' (1 John 5:13). Again and again he emphasises the same great note of assurance: 'We *know* that we have come to know him' (1 John 2:3); 'This is how we *know* we are in him' (1 John 2:5); 'We *know* that we have passed from death to life' (1 John 3:14); 'we *know* that we belong to the truth' (1 John 3:19); 'we *know* that he lives in us' (1 John 3:24); 'We *know* that we live in him and he in us' (1 John 4:13); 'We *know* that we are children of God' (1 John 5:19). John was not like some so-called Christians, who seem convinced about their doubts, and doubtful about their convictions! John was *sure*, he *knew*, and he longed that other Christians should share the same happy assurance about their standing. The Bible tells us that we both *can*, and *should*!

### *Jesus is alive!*

One of the most important things to realise about

assurance is that it is objective rather than subjective, in other words it is based first and foremost on things outside of ourselves. Christian assurance is more than feelings, or hopes, or longings; it is a conviction based on certainties. Take this question, for instance: I am putting my trust in Jesus Christ, but how can I *know* that my sins are forgiven, and that God will not hold me accountable for them any more? The answer to that question is this: *Jesus is alive!* Years ago, men owing money in this country were sentenced to terms of imprisonment in what were known as 'debtors' prisons'. If the debtor could not be traced, his guarantor could be sent to prison in his place. Now imagine that I had run away after contracting an unpayable debt, and that my guarantor had been jailed. Later, on passing through my home town, I saw my guarantor walking down the road, a free man. What would that tell me? It would tell me that the debt must have been paid, that all the demands of justice against me had been met, and that I too was a free man. My assurance would be based on the fact that the one who took responsibility for my debt had been released from prison; and the Christian's assurance of salvation rests on the fact that the Lord Jesus Christ, who undertook to pay the death penalty for his sin, has been released from death's prison! This is sure and certain proof that, in the Bible's own words '(God) forgave us all our sins, having cancelled the written code, with its regulations, that was against us and that stood opposed to us; he took it away, nailing it to the cross' (Colossians 2:13—14). God will not condemn those for whom Christ has already paid the death penalty, and nobody else can, for as Paul puts it 'Who will bring any charge against those whom God has chosen? It is God who justifies. Who is he that condemns? Christ Jesus, who died — more than that, who was raised to life — is at the right hand of God and is also interceding for us' (Romans 8:33—34).

## The Lord's own signature

The second great fact on which a Christian can base his assurance is that God keeps his word. The Bible teaches us that 'it is impossible for God to lie' (Hebrews 6:18) and adds that 'no matter how many promises God has made, they are "Yes" in Christ' (2 Corinthians 1:20). Now the greatest promise in the Bible is that those who put their trust in Jesus Christ are saved for ever. This promise is repeated throughout the New Testament. Here is just one instance, which surely puts the question beyond all possible doubt. Telling the Jews that he alone could give people the gift of eternal life, Jesus said 'I tell you the truth, whoever hears my word and believes him who sent me *has* eternal life and *will not* be condemned; he *has* crossed over from death to life' (John 5:24).

Here is a clear promise made by the Son of God, and recorded in the Word of God, which can be relied upon without reservation by the people of God.

In 1798, a band of armed men terrorised County Wexford, in Eire, plundering homes, and murdering local farmers. The Viceroy, Lord Cornwallis, was determined to try to turn these outlaws into useful, law-abiding citizens, and in order to do so, he made what seemed at the time to be a fantastic offer. He bought a certain field, and announced that any rebel, whatever his record might be, who stepped into that field and laid down his weapons would receive a full pardon. At first, the rebels did not believe it; it must be a trap. Finally, one of the worst of the gang decided to risk his life on the promise being true. He walked into the field, threw down his weapons, and waited anxiously for the result. A few minutes later, a soldier appeared, asked the man his name, wrote it on a piece of paper, and handed the document to him. When he looked at it, the rebel saw that the soldier had written his name on an official act of pardon which already bore the signature of Lord Cornwallis. He was a free man the moment he entered that field; he was *sure* that he was free when he saw Lord Cornwallis's signature on a pardon bearing his own name. Eventually many other rebels followed his example, and the whole area was transformed as a result. If anyone had later threatened them with arrest, all they would need to do would be to produce their signed pardons, and no charge could be brought against them. In a much more wonderful way, the Christian is saved by trusting Christ, and he can be *sure* that he is saved by knowing the great promises of salvation contained in the Bible, the promises that bear the Lord's own signature. The blood of Christ makes the Christian safe; the Word of God makes him sure!

## The Spirit's own voice

In the last chapter, when we were studying the truth about adoption, we looked at a very important passage in Romans 8, and we need to look at it again now, because it gives yet another biblical basis for assurance of salvation. Paul says that when, by the Holy Spirit, 'we cry "*Abba*, Father", the Spirit testifies with our Spirit that we are God's children' (Romans 8:16). Like all the deepest things of the human heart, this is almost impossible to describe in words, but let me ask you these questions. Do you know what it is to feel God's presence in prayer? Do you sense that you truly love God? Do you at the same time have a deep sense in your own heart that he loves you? Do you really mean what you are saying when you call him 'Father'? Do you know what it is to find your heart going out to him in love, worship, praise, thanksgiving, joy, and a sense of belonging to him? If you do, then these convictions (they are deeper than mere feelings) are the result of the Holy Spirit's work within you. They are the areas in which, as Paul puts it, the Spirit himself bears witness (the phrase means confirms, or testifies) with your own spirit that you are a child of God. When you come to God in true worship, you are not just following a mechanical formula or a religious routine, you are enjoying one of the great privileges of your spiritual relationship with your heavenly Father and, even as you worship, the Holy Spirit assures you that that relationship is real.

## Take no chances

There is all the difference in the world between assurance and presumption. For instance, it is *not* presumptuous to believe the straightforward truths of God's Word that 'Whoever believes in the Son has eternal life' (John 3:36), but it *is* presumptuous for a person to take it for granted that he is a Christian whether or not his own beliefs or behaviour in any way measure up to what the Bible lays down. Take no chances here! Peter urges the Christians of his day – and ours – to 'be all the more eager to make your calling and election sure' (2 Peter 1:10). Self-deception is dangerously possible here, but God has given us certain biblical tests, and these help us to check the reality of our Christian profession.

## The things I believe

The first of these tests is whether I believe what the Bible has to say about Jesus. The Apostle John wrote

'Dear Friends, do not believe every spirit, but test the spirits to see whether they are from God, because many false prophets have gone out into the world. This is how you can recognise the Spirit of God: Every spirit that acknowledges that Jesus Christ has come in the flesh is from God, but every spirit that does not acknowledge Jesus is not from God'. (1 John 4:1—3). Jesus was even more explicit when he told some of his critics, 'if you do not believe that I am the one I claim to be you will indeed die in your sins' (John 8:24). However well-meaning he may be, and whatever the quality of his life, no man can claim to be a Christian unless he acknowledges the deity of Christ. This is the fundamental imperative of Christianity.

## The way I behave

Here we have the other side of the coin, or the other half of the test. The reality of a person's claim to be a Christian can be checked not only by what he believes but by the way in which he behaves. Paul writes about certain people 'They claim to know God, *but by their actions deny him'* (Titus 1:16). Make a note of that! This is the area where self-deception is so easy. James says 'Do not merely listen to the word, and so deceive yourselves. Do what it says' (James 1:22). When a person becomes a true Christian, a revolution takes place, in belief and behaviour. The Bible is quite definite about it — 'Therefore, if anyone is in Christ, he is a new creation; the old has gone, the new has come!' (2 Corinthians 5:17). This does not mean that a Christian suddenly becomes perfect (we shall look at this more closely in the next chapter), but that just as earthly parents can expect physical development in their children, so we can expect to see a gradual and growing change in the life of a true child of God. It is interesting to notice how often, in that first letter of his, John links assurance with behaviour. Let us check some of the quotations we looked at before, this time widening them to include some other very significant words. For instance, John says 'We know that we have come to know (God) *if we obey his commands'* (1 John 2:3). Again, 'We know that we have passed from death to life, *because we love our brothers*' (1 John 3:14). Two verses later, he writes 'But *if anyone obeys his word,* God's love is truly made complete in him. This is how we know we are in him: Whoever claims to live in him must walk as Jesus did' (1 John 2:5–6). Finally, he says 'Dear children, *let us not love with words or tongue, but with actions and in truth.* This then is how we know that we belong to the truth, and how we set our hearts at rest in his presence whenever our hearts condemn us' (1 John 3:18–20).

From all of these statements, one clear truth emerges: the man who claims to be a Christian because he believes certain things to be true about Christ, but whose behaviour is not gladly based on the Word of God, is deceiving himself. Now apply the test to yourself! Are you honestly and earnestly seeking to be obedient to God's revealed will? Do you take the Bible as your unquestioned standard in moral and spiritual doctrine and behaviour? Are you making any progress in holy living? Are you gaining any new victories? Are you overcoming any old sinful habits? Do you long in your heart of hearts to become more and more like Jesus in your thoughts, words and actions? These are the critical tests, and the professing Christian should face up to them very carefully. Paul once wrote to the Christians at Corinth, 'Examine yourselves to see whether you are in the faith; test yourselves' (2 Corinthians 13:5). That remains a searching responsibility for all who profess to be Christians today.

# LIVING THE CHRISTIAN LIFE

# Four — Pleasing my Father

## 9. SANCTIFICATION

We turn now from the doctrinal section of our studies which we called '*Learning* the Christian Life', to the practical section, which we are calling '*Living* the Christian Life'. But this does not mean that we can forget about doctrine in order to concentrate on Christian living. When teaching his disciples, Jesus said 'Now that you *know* these things, you will be blessed if you *do* them' (John 13:17). Learning and living go together; creed and conduct are linked; belief and behaviour are firmly joined, both in the Bible and in Christian living today.

### Separate and Holy

We need to begin this chapter by understanding the meaning of the word 'sanctification'. Basically the verb 'to sanctify' or 'to make holy' has two meanings — firstly, to separate or to set aside; and secondly, to cleanse from sin, or to purify. In its first sense, it is used in the Old Testament about a great variety of things. For instance, in the story of creation we are told that 'God blessed the seventh day, and *made it holy*' (Genesis 2:3), while in a very significant ceremony, Moses '*consecrated* Aaron and his garments and his sons and their garments' (Leviticus 8:30). In neither case was the thing sanctified made any *better*; it was merely set apart in some special way.

The second use of the word comes mainly in the New Testament, where its meaning is again very clear. Paul writes 'It is God's will that you should be holy' (1 Thessalonians 4:3), adding a few verses later 'For God did not call us to be impure, but to live a holy life' (1 Thessalonians 4:7). Towards the end of the same letter he writes 'May God himself, the God of peace, sanctify you through and through. May your whole spirit, soul and body be kept blameless at the coming of our Lord Jesus Christ' (1 Thessalonians 5:23). Used in this sense, sanctification means holiness, purity of living, godliness – the vocation of every Christian in the world. We could sum up the Bible's moral demands in this one sentence: 'Be holy, because I am holy' (1 Peter 1:16). Every Christian has a responsibility to seek to obey that commandment every day of his life!

## Perfect and partial

In seeking to live the Christian life, nothing is more important than making sure that our doctrine of sanctification is *biblical*. This is especially true for young Christians, who are perhaps more likely than other people to get carried away with extravagant teaching on the subject. If you want a general rule-of-thumb, I would say this: beware of any kind of teaching about sanctification that emphasises morbid self-examination, spiritual superiority, or emotionalism. After all, Jesus was utterly holy, yet without a trace of any of these things. When Paul preached in the synagogue at Berea, we are told that they not only 'received the message with great eagerness', but that they also 'examined the Scriptures every day to see if what Paul said was true' (Acts 17:11). If they did that with the teachings of an Apostle, you would be well advised to do the same with the opinions of any lesser man! Now the Bible teaches that for the Christian, sanctification is both perfect and partial. Impossible? Certainly not! Think of a two-year-old child. Physically, he may be perfect. He is a complete human being. He needs nothing else in order to make him a member of the human race. But he is far from being fully developed. If he is going to reach mature manhood, those cells, muscles, limbs and ligaments will have to grow. The same is true in the Christian life. Paul addresses one of his New Testament letters 'To the church of God in Corinth, to those *sanctified* in Christ Jesus and *called to be holy*' (1 Corinthians 1:2). Notice how both meanings of sanctification are contained in that one verse. In the first place, Paul says that these Christians are *already sanctified.* They have been set apart by God, who no longer sees them as ungodly sinners, deserving of eternal punishment. Instead, all of the perfect righteousness of the Lord Jesus Christ is imputed to the Christian. Theologians call this 'positional holiness', because this is the position in which every Christian stands in God's sight as far as his acceptance and salvation are concerned. In this sense, sanctification is not something towards which the Christian *aims,* it is the position from which he *starts!* Because he is 'in Christ', God accepts him as if he were *perfect* in every way.

But notice that Paul says that these Christians, already 'sanctified in Christ', were also 'called to be holy'. In this sense, their sanctification was only *partial.* They could not sit back and rest on the fact that God reckoned them as perfect; they were called to do everything in their power to ensure that their daily lives were holy, clean, pure, pleasing to God. The writer of the Epistle to the Hebrews urges his readers, 'Make every effort . . . to be holy', adding that 'without holiness no one will see the Lord' (Hebrews 12:14). For the Christian, sanctification, or holiness of life, is something that must be pursued every day, in every situation, and by every means at his disposal.

## A walking civil war

As we saw in an earlier chapter, the Bible teaches that when a person becomes a Christian, he receives a new nature through the indwelling of the Holy Spirit. But the Bible also teaches that the old nature remains, even the Apostle Paul frankly admitting 'I know that nothing good lives in me, that is, in my sinful nature' (Romans 7:18). The result is that man is a kind of walking civil war, with the two natures, the old and the new, fighting for the upper hand. Notice how Paul goes on to say that 'in my inner being I delight in God's law; but I see another law at work in the members of my body, waging war against the law of my mind' (Romans 7:22–23). Writing to the Galatians, he spells it out even more clearly: 'For the sinful nature desires what is contrary to the Spirit, and the Spirit what is contrary to the sinful nature. They are in conflict with each other' (Galatians 5:17). When the Bible speaks about the need for a Christian to be sanctified, it is speaking about the gradual putting to death of the old nature and the growing control of the new.

## Means to an end

Now that we have seen something of the meaning of sanctification, it is vitally important to grasp another biblical truth: no Christian is capable of becoming holy in his own strength. A man is just as incapable of living a holy life as he is of saving himself in the first place, but with this important difference. Whereas the new birth is a sovereign work of God the Holy Spirit, in which man has no part at all, sanctification is something in which the Christian is called upon to co-operate with the Holy Spirit. Peter tells his readers that '(God's) divine power has given us everything we need for life and godliness', but then adds, a verse or two later, *'For this very reason, make every effort* to add to your faith, goodness; and to goodness, knowledge; and to knowledge, self-control; and to self-control, perseverance; and to perseverance, godliness; and to godliness, brotherly kindness; and to brotherly kindness, love' (2 Peter 1:3, 5–7). In other words, God has provided all the means for us to live holy lives; it is our responsibility to use them.

### The Father's will

As we have already seen, the Bible says plainly 'it is God's will that you should be holy' (1 Thessalonians 4:3). To know that is the starting-point for the Christian as he sets out to live a holy life. Jesus was able to sum up his entire life of obedience to his Father in heaven by saying 'I always do what pleases him' (John 8:29), and this should be the aim of the Christian. The more we know of the majesty, the holiness, the power, the glory, and the love of God, the more concerned we shall be that we please him in every part of our lives. When Joseph was tempted to commit adultery with Potiphar's wife, his reply was immediate and clear — 'How then could I do such a wicked thing and sin against God?' (Genesis 39:9). The Christian should take exactly the same attitude in the face of every temptation to sin.

### The Saviour's death

The Bible says that 'we have been made holy through the sacrifice of the body of Jesus Christ once for all'

(Hebrews 10:10). This obviously refers to that perfect sanctification which we were studying earlier. The 'once for all' sacrifice of Christ means that God no longer takes our sin into account as far as our relationship to him is concerned. But the fact that Christ went to such tremendous lengths to save us from the consequences of our sin should surely be a powerful incentive to live a life of holiness. How can a Christian gladly consent to sin when looking at the cross of his Saviour? The more the death of Christ means to the Christian, the less he wants to sin. The writer of the letter to the Hebrews tells us that when people profess to be Christians and then turn back into open sin, 'they are crucifying the Son of God all over again, and subjecting him to public disgrace' (Hebrews 6:6). No true Christian will want to have any part in that!

## The Spirit's work

Here again, the Bible speaks of both perfect and partial sanctification. After describing various kinds of ungodly men, Paul tells the Corinthians, 'And that is what some of you were. But you were washed, you were sanctified, you were justified in the name of the Lord Jesus Christ and by the Spirit of our God' (1 Corinthians 6:11). He is telling these Christians that at the time of their conversion, God set them apart, justified them, and made them his own, and that this was the work of the Holy Spirit. But in writing to the Galatians he says 'live by the Spirit, and you will not gratify the desires of the sinful nature' (Galatians 5:16), while he tells the Romans that it is 'by the Spirit' that they are to 'put to death the misdeeds of the body' (Romans 8:13). Here, of course, he is referring to partial, or gradual, sanctification, and he says that this, too, is possible only through the power of the

Holy Spirit. Without the Holy Spirit, no man could keep clear of sin even for a moment; with the Holy Spirit, a Christian has the marvellous potential of avoiding sin and of living a life that is pleasing to God. As we saw in an earlier chapter, the Christian's real potential for holy living comes from the fact that 'it is God who works in you to will and to act according to his good purpose' (Philippians 2:13).

## The word of truth

The greatest instrument used by the Holy Spirit in making a Christian holy is the Bible itself. He takes its warnings, its promises, its examples, its truths, and its motives, and makes them 'live' to the Christian, drawing him on to new dimensions of discipleship and obedience. The Bible is full of statements that show how important its teachings are in the life of the Christian. The psalmist asks 'How can a young man keep his way pure?' and then answers 'By living according to your word' (Psalm 119:9). Later on in the same Psalm he says 'Your word is a lamp to my feet and a light for my path' (Psalm 119:105). Praying for his disciples, and for all succeeding generations of Christians, Jesus asks his heavenly Father to 'Sanctify them by the truth; your word is truth' (John 17:17). When he was being subjected to a tremendous battering of temptation by Satan, Jesus retaliated by standing on the truth of God's word, and three times he beat back the enemy on the basis of being able to say 'It is written . . .' (Matthew 4:4, 7, 10). We shall have a separate chapter on the Bible, but for the moment be sure to get a grasp of this: the defeated Christian is almost without exception the Christian who is neglecting his Bible. The victorious Christian is the Christian who is able to say that 'his delight is in the law of

the Lord, and on his law he meditates day and night'
(Psalm 1:2).

## Power through prayer

Prayer also warrants a chapter on its own, and we shall
come to it later, but we must just mention it here,
because it obviously plays a part in almost every other
'means' of sanctification. In prayer the Christian can
not only come to God in worship, praise, adoration,
and thanksgiving, but he can also ask for daily and
specific help to understand the truth of the Bible, to
resist temptation, and to follow after holiness. In
Isaiah's words, 'those who hope in the Lord will renew
their strength. They will soar on wings like eagles;
they will run and not grow weary, they will walk and
not be faint' (Isaiah 40:31). And to that graphic statement by an Old Testament prophet, we can add this
punchy phrase from a New Testament apostle — 'The
prayer of a righteous man is powerful and effective'
(James 5:16). The Christian gains power through
prayer!

## A living faith

Amongst many other things, the Bible describes the
Christian life as a race, and in one of the places it uses
this simile it adds another essential element in the
Christian's sanctification. The writer of Hebrews, after
listing a procession of men and women who had lived
triumphantly for God, says 'Therefore, since we are
surrounded by such a great cloud of witnesses, let us
throw off everything that hinders and the sin that so
easily entangles, and let us run with perseverance the
race marked out for us. *Let us fix our eyes on Jesus,*
the author and perfecter of our faith' (Hebrews 12:
1–2). What the Apostle is calling for here is *faith,* a

continuing conviction of the presence of Jesus, of the faithfulness of his promises, and of his power at work within us by the Holy Spirit. While a Christian has a responsibility to exercise discipline, to pray, to read God's word, to resist temptation, and to strive after holiness, it is nevertheless true that he will only be successful as he develops and deepens his living faith in Christ. Paul had no doubts about that: 'I have been crucified with Christ and I no longer live, but Christ lives in me. The life I live in the body, *I live by faith in the Son of God,* who loved me and gave himself for me' (Galatians 2:20). This principle is overwhelmingly confirmed as you read that list of godly men and women I mentioned a moment ago. In the 39 verses of Hebrews 11, the writer mentions faith no fewer than 24 times! It was the one great factor that was common to all of these people. They were men and women of *faith*; and no Christian will make progress in holiness unless he keeps his eyes firmly fixed on Jesus, trusting him for forgiveness, power, wisdom and guidance. Whereas even the weakest faith can bring salvation to a man in a moment of time, it takes strong, constant faith to make him holy. In looking at Jesus, a glance can save, but only a gaze can sanctify!

## The finished product

In living the Christian life, there is no such thing as finality. No matter how far you may travel along the road of holiness, or how near you may live to Christ, or how many victories you may gain over sin of many kinds, the fact remains that final deliverance, not only from the penalty and power of sin, but also from its presence, will not be yours until you get to heaven. There is no experience, or crisis, or gift that can put you in the position where you will enter into what some people call 'sinless perfection'. No Christian is ever wholly free from sin — not even those who claim to be, or who say that such a thing is possible. The old, fallen nature remains with us right until the end of our earthly journey. Never be tempted to think that you can achieve in a moment's crisis what God has said can only happen by a lifetime's process. Writing to the Philippians about being conformed to Christ, Paul adds *'Not that I have already obtained all this, or have already been made perfect,* but I press on to take hold of that for which Christ Jesus took hold of me' (Philippians 3:12). If the Apostle Paul, towards the end of his remarkable life, acknowledged that he was by no means perfect, you can safely ignore the extravagant claims of any present-day enthusiasts who claim to have gone one better! *But we will be perfect one day!* The process of the Christian's sanctification will come to a glorious climax in heaven. God's eternal purpose that Christians should be 'conformed to the likeness of (God's) Son' (Romans 8:29) will be realised. Our longing to be like Christ will be completely satisfied when 'we shall be like him, for we shall see him as he is' (1 John 3:2). And when that happens, and we stand in God's presence 'as a radiant church, without stain or wrinkle or any other blemish, but holy and blameless' (Ephesians 5:27), all the struggles, and effort, and tears, and pressures, and praying and discipline, and suffering will have been more than worthwhile! Paul's words to the Christians at Corinth help us to get it in perspective — 'Though outwardly we are wasting away, yet inwardly we are being renewed day by day. For our light and momentary troubles are achieving for us an eternal glory that far outweighs them all' (2 Corinthians 4:16—17).

# 10. SERVICE

One of the clearest New Testament descriptions of what it is to be a Christian comes in Paul's first letter to the Thessalonians. He told them that people all over Macedonia and Achaia knew of their faith in God, and goes on — 'Therefore we do not need to say anything about it, for they themselves report what kind of reception you gave us. They tell how you *turned* to God from idols *to serve* the living and true God' (1 Thessalonians 1:8—9). Notice the words I have emphasised! Morally, a Christian is called to sanctification; dynamically, he is called to service.

## Everybody in!

People sometimes ask me when I began full-time Christian service. When they do, I am tempted to ask them to re-phrase the question — because what they are *really* asking is 'When did you resign from your position in the Civil Service and devote the whole of your time to preaching?' — and the two questions are not the same! It is an example of the way in which a casual use of words can lead us into faulty thinking. Let me demonstrate what I mean by answering both questions in one sentence. I began the particular work in which I am now engaged in 1962, but I began full-time Christian service eight years earlier, *on the day I was converted.* As Paul's word to the Thessalonians makes absolutely clear, Christians are those who turn from their idols *'to serve the living and true God'.* He implied exactly the same basic truth when addressing his terrified companions on board their stricken ship off the Mediterranean island of Clauda, speaking of 'the God whose I am, and whom I serve' (Acts 27:23). As far as Paul was concerned, his position was absolutely clear: he was both God's property and God's servant. The implications for you and for me are worth noting very carefully!

### There can be no release from Christian service

When an industrial strike is called, the shop steward's cry is 'Everybody out!'; but in Christian service the cry is 'Everybody in!' *Every* Christian is called upon 'to serve the living and true God', and in God's service there are no part-timers, no 'temps', no half-days or holidays, no early closing, no provision for strikes, lock-outs, sit-ins or working to rule — and no retirement!

### There must be no compromise in Christian service

There is no such thing as free-lance work in the Kingdom of God, nor must a Christian even consider the possibility of having a 'second string' or a 'sideline'. Jesus said plainly that 'No one can serve two masters' (Matthew 6:24), with the obvious implication that he must serve one. In yielding himself to Christ, the Christian has made his choice as to whom that one shall be.

### There should be no reservations in Christian service

It has been said that while the entrance fee into the Kingdom of God is nothing, the annual subscription is everything, and this is certainly true in terms of Christian service. To be a Christian is to be committed to doing the revealed will of God — nothing more, nothing less, and nothing else — for the whole of my life. My service may not be perfect, but I must see to it that I am able to say with the Apostle Paul that God is the one 'whom I serve with my whole heart' (Romans 1:9).

## The master servant

But where can the Christian turn to find a perfect example of a servant of God? To Abraham, or Moses, or David, or Paul, or Peter, or John? No! — because whilst we can certainly learn a great deal from the record of their lives, they were all eclipsed by the greatest servant of all — Jesus!

When John pointed Jesus out as 'the Lamb of God, who takes away the sin of the world!' (John 1:29), the Jews would immediately have recognised this as a statement that Jesus was the promised Messiah who was to replace all the animal sacrifices made under the Old Covenant. But some of them would have grasped another great truth, because the Aramaic word for 'lamb' is also the word for 'servant', and they would have linked this with parts of Isaiah's prophecy which spoke of deliverance coming to Israel through the one whom God called 'my servant' (Isaiah 52:13). And if there was any doubt about the matter, Jesus removed it by saying plainly in the course of his ministry, 'For even the Son of Man did not come to be served, but to serve, and to give his life as a ransom for many' (Mark 10:45). His life on earth was seen in terms of service, and as his service was perfect, it was of course marked by perfect obedience.

This fundamental truth about the life of Jesus being one of obedient service is underlined throughout the Bible. In one of his great Psalms, David says 'To do your will, O my God, is my desire; your law is within my heart' (Psalm 40:8). But if you look up Hebrews 10:5—7, you will see that these words were also applied to Jesus, whose coming into the world to put away sin was in obedience to his heavenly Father's will. When, on one occasion, his disciples wondered what he meant by saying 'I have food to eat that you know nothing about', Jesus replied 'My food is to do the will of him who sent me, and to finish his work' (John 4:32, 34). As he neared the end of his earthly life, he looked into his Father's face and said 'I have brought you glory on earth by completing the work you gave me to do' (John 17:4). Finally, as he hung on the cross, his last triumphant cry was 'It is finished' (John 19:30). Total, uncompromising obedience was the hall-mark of Jesus, the master servant: every Christian is called to follow his example.

## The Master's service

Because Jesus was the perfect servant, the Gospels teem with the excellence of his example and the truth of his teaching. Let us just look at one thing he said about his own service, and notice how much it has to tell us about Christian service in general. In the course of healing a man blind from birth, Jesus told his disciples 'As long as it is day we must do the work of him who sent me. Night is coming, when no one can work' (John 9:4). That one small sentence contains three principles vital for all Christian service. Let us look at each of them briefly.

### *Firstly, the necessity of Christian service*

Jesus said 'We *must* do the work ...' There was a kind of irrestistible compulsion about everything Jesus did. He told Zaccheus 'I *must* stay at your house today' (Luke 19:5); in a prophecy concerning his death, he told Nicodemus 'the Son of Man *must* be lifted up' (John 3:14); telling the Jews that Gentiles, too, would enter the Kingdom of God, he said 'I *must* bring them also' (John 10:16); he explained to his disciples that 'he *must* go to Jerusalem and suffer many things at the hands of the elders, chief priests and teachers of the law and that he *must* be killed and on the third day be raised to life' (Matthew 16:21). Yet these 'musts' were not the pressure of an outward law, but the pressure of an inward love; he *delighted* to do his Father's will. Nothing is more foreign to Christianity than idleness; a lazy Christian is almost a contradiction in terms. This is how Paul puts it — 'Be very careful, then, how you live — not as unwise but as wise, making the most of every opportunity, because the days are evil' (Ephesians 5:15—16). For the spiritual Christian time is not something to be *spent*, but to be *bought*, and gladly used in the service of his Lord and Master.

*Secondly, the authority of Christian service*

Jesus spoke of 'the work of him who sent me'. We have already noticed how often he said the same kind of thing, and it was all crystallised in that one great moment in the Garden of Gethsemane when he cried 'Father, if you are willing, take this cup from me; yet *not my will, but yours be done*' (Luke 22:42). As perfect man, he submitted his will without reservation to the higher will of his heavenly father. The great characteristic of his life was not its busyness, but its obedience, and the really startling thing was not the power he displayed, but the authority he claimed for what he did. His whole life moved along the lines of God's perfect will, and that was the great open secret of its joy, its freedom and its effectiveness. There is a great lesson here for every Christian. Beware of confusing busyness with obedience. Some of the most frustrated, ineffective Christians in the world are those who never have a moment to spare. They dash here and there in a great lather of excitement, getting involved up to their necks in every form of Christian service that comes their way – but at the end of the day they seem to have little or nothing to show for all their expenditure of time, money, energy and resources. Why? Because they have plunged headlong into things without ever pausing to discover whether or not any particular form of service was God's will for them. I have always been impressed by the way in which Luke so faithfully records that 'Paul and his companions travelled throughout the region of Phrygia and Galatia, having been kept by the Holy Spirit from preaching the word in the province of Asia' and goes on to say 'When they came to the border of Mysia, they tried to enter Bithynia, but the Spirit of Jesus would not allow them to' (Acts 16:6–7). Yet a few verses later Luke records that after a remarkable vision given to Paul, 'we got ready at once to leave for Macedonia, concluding that God had called us to preach the gospel to them' (Acts 16:10). Now these men were under orders to 'preach the good news to all creation' (Mark 16:15) – yet the Holy Spirit clearly *prevented* them from preaching in some areas, and *persuaded* them to preach in others. Only when they were clear as to God's specific will in the matter could they go forward with confidence. Take careful note of that! If the devil cannot make you into a lazy Christian, he will make you into a busy one outside of God's will – and that is another, subtler form of disobedience. Nothing is right for a Christian if it is not God's will for him, even when it seems commendable. Thomas Barnado volunteered to go to China as a medical missionary; if he had insisted on going he would have missed God's will for his life, his wonderful work amongst needy children. Only service done by God's authority can possibly have his approval. Many Christians would do a lot more if they did a lot less – provided that that 'lot less' was directed by the Spirit of God. Learn the secret of discovering God's will before you try to do it!

### *Thirdly, the urgency of Christian service*

Jesus made it clear that our opportunity to work for God here on earth would last only 'As long as it is day'. While it is true that frantic, unguided Christian service often does more harm than good, it is also true that a genuine note of urgency runs through everything that the Bible has to say about the Christian's work for God. The most obvious factor is, of course, that man's time on earth is limited. The day is coming when 'The heavens will disappear with a roar; the elements will be destroyed by fire, and the earth and everything in it will be laid bare' (2 Peter 3:10). Things will not go on for ever as they are at present. The moment will come when God calls a halt to man's era of time-and-space existence — *and no man knows when that will be.* What we do know is that 'now is the time of God's favour, now is the day of salvation' (2 Corinthians 6:2). We have all the time in the world to serve the Lord — but how much time does the world have?

Another obvious factor that makes our Christian service urgent is that we ourselves are frail, finite creatures, with just one brief lifetime in which to work. The Bible says that David 'served God's purpose in his own generation' (Acts 13:36) — and it was the only generation he could serve! You will not be a teenager, or a student, or a farmer, or a businessman, or a housewife, *for ever*! Whatever opportunity you have for serving the Lord at this moment is a *passing* opportunity — it is limited by your uncertain lifespan, and possibly by other factors too. To continue that line of thought even further, the Bible makes the final, inescapable point when it says 'Now listen, you who say, "Today or tomorrow we will go to this or that city, spend a year there, carry on business and make money!" Why, you do not even know what will happen tomorrow. What is your life? You are a mist that appears for a little while and then vanishes' (James 4:13—14). Nothing could make the urgency of Christian service clearer than that! It is not only the road to hell that is paved with good intentions — so, for some people, is the road to heaven! Learn to balance the need for seeking God's will for your Christian service with the determination that you will serve him with a deep, solemn sense of the urgency of all that you do. Watching a baseball game on American television once, I was told that the ball is in a hittable position for only about one-twohundredth of a second! If the batter failed to make contact then he would not make a clean and effective hit. Dynamic Christian service is when a person knows God's will — and then does it with all his heart.

## The Greeks had a word for it

Almost everything we have looked at in this chapter so far centres around the English verb 'to serve'. Yet in our present context the words 'servant' and 'service' in our English versions of the New Testament are used to translate at least six different words in the Greek original. Each of these words has its own peculiar shade of meaning, and each can tell us some specific thing about the characteristics we should aim at in our life's work for God. Let us look at them briefly in turn.

### First, enthusiasm

The Greek word is *leitourgos,* from which we get our English word — 'liturgy'. Among the Greeks generally it was used of a man who undertook some work for the State at his own expense, suggesting generosity and enthusiasm. Paul uses it when commending the Corinthians for their generous gifts. He says that 'This *service* that you perform is not only supplying the needs of God's people but is also overflowing in many expressions of thanks to God' (2 Corinthians 9:12). Every Christian should be an irrepressible enthusiast about his Saviour and about his service for him!

## Second, dignity

The Greek word is *therapon*. It is a word that speaks of dignity, freedom and honour. The Bible says that 'Moses was faithful as a *servant* in all God's house, testifying to what would be said in the future' (Hebrews 3:5). Moses held a unique position in the Old Testament, yet his dignity came not from his position, but from 'God's house'. Paul tells the Corinthians 'For we are God's fellow workers' (1 Corinthians 3:9), and in doing so gives every obedient Christian a position of high honour. Those engaged in God's service are 'Christ's ambassadors' (2 Corinthians 5:20), not third rate messenger-boys!

## Third, humility

The Greek word is *huperetes,* which literally means 'an under-rower'. The picture is of a person not taking the lead, but content to serve faithfully in a lowly position. Paul tells the Corinthians 'So then, men ought to regard us as *servants* of Christ and as those entrusted with the secret things of God' (1 Corinthians 4:1). Although the Christian servant holds a dignified office, he must never be arrogant or proud about it. Whatever his particular task, he remains an 'under-rower', or, if you like, second violin; and it takes a great deal of grace to play the second fiddle well! Beware of the danger of becoming too big for God to use!

## Fourth, perseverance

The Greek word is *latris,* which means a hired servant, one working for wages, and therefore not allowed to take time off. It is the word used about the Christians in heaven who stand round about God's throne and '*serve* him day and night in his temple' (Revelation 7:15). The New Testament picture of a Christian servant is not of a person who has flashes of enthusiasm, followed by long periods of apathy, but rather of someone who is steady, reliable and trustworthy. Which picture gives the best likeness of you?

## Fifth, obedience

The Greek word is *diakonos,* from which we get our English word 'deacon'. The word is more closely connected to the doing of the work than to the holding of the office, and is probably connected with the verb *dioko,* which means 'to run after, or pursue'. In his greetings at the end of his letter to the Romans, Paul says 'I commend to you our sister Phoebe, a *servant* of the church in Cenchrea' (Romans 16:1) — but the important thing to notice is that it is used in the New Testament of so many people and of so many different kinds of service. It is used as a title for Jesus, for the apostles, and for anonymous and unknown Christians; it describes preaching, prison visitation, administrative duties, and general unspecified work in backing up the ministry of those who were in the front line of evangelism. There is a vitally important truth here! Everywhere in the New Testament the important thing is not prominence, but obedience. The Bible condemns the attitude that sends men chasing after titles, positions, and honours. It abhors men's deadly determination to be President of this, Chairman of that and Secretary of the other. Notice what Jesus had to say about this kind of thing: 'You know that those who are regarded as rulers of the Gentiles lord it over them, and their high officials exercise authority over them. Not so with you. Instead, whoever wants to become great among you must be your servant, and whoever wants to be first must be slave of all' (Mark 10:42—44). The holding of an office does not give us the right to be officious! To perform the lowliest task in society, or in the church, in a spirit of humble obedience, is more commendable, and will receive greater reward than to hold the highest office in either in a spirit of pride and self-seeking.

### Sixth, devotion

The Greek word is *doulos*, which literally means a bondslave, and it is the most common of all of these New Testament words. Paul calls himself 'a *servant* of Christ Jesus (Romans 1:1) and uses the word again and again to emphasise the very essence of Christian service. It is a very strong word, suggesting nothing less than complete and utter bondage, yet in Christian use it means a bondage that is spontaneous, voluntary, joyful and whole-hearted. What is more, it does not describe service rendered to a cause, a programme, or an organisation, but always and entirely to a person, the Lord Jesus Christ. Finally, that service is rendered not with the hope of receiving something, but in response to something already received. As Paul tells the Corinthians, 'Christ's love compels us' (2 Corinthians 5:14). All of a Christian's service is to be offered in the light of the amazing love of the one who, as Paul says in the very next verse, 'died for all that those who live should no longer live for themselves, but for him who died for them and was raised again' (2 Corinthians 5:15). Make sure that you see your service for the Lord (in other words, the whole of your life) not just in terms of duty, but of devotion. When Samuel was giving one of his great 'state of the nation' messages to the people of Israel, he ended by urging them to 'be sure to fear the Lord and serve him faithfully with all your heart; consider what great things he has done for you' (1 Samuel 12:24). No Christian should settle for less!

## 11. WATCHFULNESS

We began the last chapter by noticing how Paul reminded the Thessalonians that they had 'turned to God from idols to serve the living and true God'; but if we had continued the quotation we would have included these words — 'and to wait for his Son from heaven, whom he raised from the dead — Jesus, who rescues us from the coming wrath' (1 Thessalonians 1:10). That brings us to one of the most fundamental, exciting and challenging doctrines in the whole Bible — the fact that Jesus Christ is going to return to the earth.

### Who knows the future?

One of the most exhilarating things about the Bible is the way in which over and over again its history is proved to be astonishingly accurate. Scientists, archaeologists and historians, far from disproving the Bible's record, have repeatedly underlined its truth. But even the verification of the Bible's history pales alongside another tremendous factor — the fulfilment of the

Bible's prophecy. For instance, many prophecies about the nation of Israel, made in the early part of the Old Testament, were fulfilled to the letter and their fulfilment recorded later in the Bible. But it is when we consider the prophecies about Jesus that the issue becomes mind-boggling. It has been calculated that there are 109 prophecies about his birth, life, teaching, death, burial, resurrection and ascension scattered throughout the Old Testament. By the Law of Compound Probabilities, the odds against all of these being fulfilled by chance are astronomical; to be precise, 6,451,444,325,125,601,253,342,971,930,704,920 to 1! Yet every single one was fulfilled to the letter in the space of 33 years. Included in these prophecies are 25 details relating to his betrayal, death and burial. The odds against these alone being fulfilled are nearly 350 million to 1, yet they were all precisely fulfilled within the space of 24 hours! Whatever clever arguments people may use in trying to disprove the miracles recorded in the Bible, they are forced into silence by these staggering facts. But that is not the end of the story. Not only does the Bible contain just over 100 prophecies about the *first* coming of Jesus into the world, the New Testament alone has about 300 references to his return, or *second* coming. Mathematically, this amounts to the subject being mentioned once for every thirteen verses from Matthew to Revelation. God knows the future — and on this issue at least he has ensured that we know too!

## Call the witnesses

If only one of the New Testament writers mentioned the second coming of Christ, but did so many times, the sceptic might argue that he had a bee in his theological bonnet — though even one mention in the

Word of God should be sufficient for the Christian! But the fact is that it is difficult to find a New Testament writer who does *not* mention the subject. Let us call the witnesses to the stand.

*Matthew* records these words of Jesus — 'For the Son of Man is going to come in his Father's glory with his angels' (Matthew 16:27).

*Mark* has the words of Jesus that men would one day 'see the Son of Man sitting at the right hand of the Mighty One and coming on the clouds of heaven' (Mark 14:62).

*Luke* includes the warning that 'the Son of Man will come at an hour when you do not expect him' (Luke 12:40).

*John* has the plainest testimony of all, the straight-forward promise of Jesus to his disciples that having prepared a place for them in heaven 'I will come back and take you to be with me that you also may be where I am' (John 14:3).

*Paul* speaks of the time when the Lord Jesus would be 'revealed from heaven in blazing fire with his power-ful angels' (2 Thessalonians 1:7).

*Peter* promises faithful Christians that 'when the Chief Shepherd appears, you will receive the crown of glory that will never fade away' (1 Peter 5:4).

*James* tells us that 'the Lord's coming is near' (James 5:8).

*The author of the letter to the Hebrews (identity uncertain)* says of Jesus that he 'was sacrificed once to take away the sins of many people; and he will appear a second time, not to bear sin, but to bring salvation to those who are waiting for him' (Hebrews 9:28).

### The wood and the trees

The second coming of Christ is part of what the theologians call eschatology, or the doctrine of the last things, a subject full of controversy and differences of opinion. Countless books have been written putting forward various points of view about the exact time-table of events that will happen when the end of the world comes, and many people have become very hot under the collar insisting that their interpretation is the only right one. The Bible has been ransacked from cover to cover to find support for details of the terminal timetable, and organisations have even been raised up with the specific purpose of emphasising one particular line of interpretation. All of this means that if you try to take in everything that is being said on the subject, you will find it very difficult to see the wood for the trees. By far the best thing to do is to keep to simple biblical guidelines. Scripture is always a better guide than even the most enthusiastic of speculations!

### The world's best-kept secret

One of the things the Bible teaches very firmly about the second coming of Christ is that no man knows exactly when it will occur. Jesus said quite clearly that 'No one knows about that day or hour, not even the angels in heaven' (Mark 13:32). Yet ever since Jesus spoke those words, men have tried to forecast the date of the end of the world. Many people felt that it would happen in the year 1000. Others said it would happen in 1260. A brilliant mathematician calculated that Jesus would return between 1688 and 1700. A Roman Catholic priest wrote a book in which he forecast that the end of the world would come in 1847, and was promptly given permission to publish the book in 1848!

The Jehovah's Witnesses have backed a whole string

of losers – 1874, 1914 and 1915, and are at present on record as expecting the end to come in 1975, the year in which this book is being written!

All of this speculation is foolish and futile. For his own perfect reasons, God has chosen to keep secret the date of Christ's return.

## Signs of the times

Although, as we have seen, no man knows the exact day, month or even year of Christ's return, the Bible does have a kind of 'early warning system', enabling us to confirm that the end is coming. When asked what would be the signs of his coming, and of the end of the world, Jesus gave several replies. Here are some of them.

### Sign number one: an increase of false teaching

'Watch out that no one deceives you. For many will come in my name, claiming "I am the Christ", and will deceive many . . . and many false prophets will appear and deceive many people' (Matthew 24:4—5, 11).

### Sign number two: violent international conflicts

'You will hear of wars and rumours of wars . . . Nation will rise against nation, and kingdom against kingdom' (Matthew 24:6—7).

### Sign number three: widespread natural disasters

'There will be famines and earthquakes in various places' (Matthew 24:7).

### Sign number four: persecution of Christians

'Then you will be handed over to be persecuted and

put to death, and you will be hated by all nations because of me' (Matthew 24:9).

*Sign number five: increasing sin and apostasy*
'Because of the increase of wickedness, the love of most will grow cold, but he who stands firm to the end will be saved' (Matthew 24:12–13).

*Sign number six: world-wide evangelism*
'And this gospel of the kingdom will be preached in the whole world as a testimony to all nations, and then the end will come' (Matthew 24:14).

Does all of this mean that Christ's return is imminent? Yes and no! It would not be difficult to show that at almost any time during the last 20 centuries one could have ticked off almost all of these 'signs', and drawn the wrong conclusion that the world was at its last gasp. Yet surely they appear even more startling in the day and age in which we now live? But whatever your interpretation, this much is certain: the return of Christ is 2,000 years nearer than when these 'signs' were first prophesied! Jesus said 'When you see these things happening you know that it is near, right at the door' (Mark 13:29). If that was true then, it is more urgently true *now*! The second coming of Christ is never a doctrine for tomorrow, but always for today. What is more, it does not merely supply information, it demands action. It is not just meant to add to our knowledge, but to affect our lives. It demands a response to one simple, searching challenge, to which we now turn.

**Are you ready?**
Many people outside of the church dismiss all talk of

Jesus coming again as sheer nonsense — but that, too, was predicted in the Bible! Peter wrote that 'in the last days scoffers will come, scoffing and following their own evil desires. They will say "Where is this 'coming' he promised? Ever since our fathers died, everything goes on as it has since the beginning of creation" ' (2 Peter 3:3–4). But for the Christian, what matters is not the voice of the sceptic, but the voice of the Saviour, and what Jesus said was this — 'What I say to you, I say to everyone: *"Watch"* ' (Mark 13:37). The challenge is simple and clear: are you on the lookout for Christ's return? Are you ready for it? This is how you can check your answer to those questions:

## You are not ready if you are lost

Jesus made it clear that his return would be a moment of dramatic separation and terrible judgment. He explained that life will be going on as normal all over the world, with people 'eating and drinking, marrying and giving in marriage' (Matthew 24:38). Then, suddenly, he will appear, and in a moment of time, 'Two men will be in the field; one will be taken and the other left. Two women will be grinding with a hand mill; one will be taken and the other left' (Matthew 24:40–41). For the Christian, it will be a moment of amazing delight, as he is taken to be with the Lord for ever; for the unbeliever, it will be a moment of agonising despair, as he realises that he will have no further opportunity to get right with God, but is doomed to spend eternity in hell. Paul says that when Jesus returns 'He will punish those who do not know God and do not obey the gospel of our Lord Jesus. They will be punished with everlasting destruction, and shut out from the presence of the Lord and from the majesty of his power on the day he comes to be glorified in his holy people and to be marvelled at among all those who have believed' (2 Thessalonians 1:8—10).

Here is the tremendous challenge that the second coming of Christ presents to the person who is lost, who has never trusted him as their personal Saviour. Are you sure where you stand on this issue? If you have never yet done so, then turn to God *now* in repentance and faith, so that if Jesus should return during your lifetime, you will be one of those taken to glory, and not one of those left to judgment.

### You are not ready if you are lukewarm

Whilst it is true that no Christian can ever fall away and be lost, the Bible also infers that many who are living on the earth when Jesus returns will be embarrassed and ashamed by his sudden appearance, because of the sub-standard quality of their lives, and their lack of loving devotion to him at that moment. John writes 'And now, dear children, continue in him, so that when he appears we may be confident and unashamed before him at his coming' (1 John 2:28). It is always embarrassing to have to meet somebody with whom you are not in happy fellowship — how much more so when that person is the Lord Jesus Christ! It is exactly here that the doctrine of the second coming is meant to motivate the Christian to godliness of life. After describing some of the global upheaval that will accompany Christ's return, with the heavens and the earth dissolving in fire, Peter asks 'Since everything will be destroyed in this way, what kind of people ought you to be? You ought to live holy and godly lives as you look forward to the day of God and speed its coming' (2 Peter 3:11—12). Would you be ashamed at your lack of devotion, at the lukewarmness of your love for him, at your compromising and backsliding, if Jesus were to return today?

### You are not ready if you are lazy

In one of his parables, Jesus likened the kingdom of God to a nobleman who went abroad for a while, but promised to return. Before leaving, he entrusted each of his servants with a certain sum of money, with clear instructions to 'Put this money to work until I come back' (Luke 19:13). In exactly the same way, God has blessed every Christian in the world with particular gifts, talents, opportunities and responsibilities – and he expects them to be used to the full until Christ returns. During my first visit to the United States I held an evangelistic Crusade at a Church in Michigan. On the opening night, the choir chose as an introit the song 'Coming again'. On the second night, to my great surprise, they opened with the same song, and then proceeded to repeat it every night throughout the week. I have never forgotten that! Whatever subject I preached on during that week, it was against the background, as it were, of the truth that Jesus is coming again; and that experience has been a constant reminder to me ever since that all of my Christian service should be done in the same context. The only way I know of being sure that I am actively involved in the Lord's service when he comes is to be involved in it *now*! The stewardship of the whole of my time must be seen in the light of the fact that the return of the Lord will be sudden, and may be soon!

Do you have the same convictions about your life, your work, your daily responsibilities? The second coming of Christ is not meant to make you frantic, but it should make you fervent: it should not produce recklessness, but it does demand carefulness: the Christian with a right view of the Bible's teaching on this great subject will learn to live, not in an attitude of wasteful desperation, but in a spirit of watchful dedication, knowing that on that day the Lord 'will reward each person according to what he has done' (Matthew 16:27).

# Five — Fighting my enemy

---

## 12. THE DEVIL

This chapter brings us face to face with the most extraordinary being in the whole universe other than God himself — the devil. To many people the devil is just a figment of theological imagination, or at most a way of describing the sum total of everything evil. To others, he is a fun figure, a cartoonist's dream, a peppery old man with red cheeks and green eyes, and with horns protruding from his head and a tail from his trousers. Yet nothing could be further from the truth, as we shall see as we turn to the Word of God.

### Aliases unlimited

As you read the Bible, you will discover that a person's name frequently gives a clue to their nature or character. To give the best possible example, the word 'Jesus' is the Greek version of the Hebrew 'Joshua', meaning 'The Lord is salvation', a perfect description of who Jesus is and what Jesus did. In the same way, we can learn a great deal about the devil by looking through the list of names the Bible uses for him. In today's society a criminal uses one or more aliases to conceal his identity; but up to date police files will record the same names in order to reveal it. In a similar way, the Bible unmasks the real nature and character of the devil by listing the names under which he operates. Here are some of them, straight from the files. To take his best-known name first, he is called 'the devil' (Matthew 4:1), a word that means an accuser, a slanderer. Then he is called 'Satan' (Job 1:6), meaning an adversary or opponent. These first two titles crop up in more revealing form elsewhere: he is specifically called 'the accuser of our brothers' (Revelation 12:10) and 'your enemy' (1 Peter 5:8). Jesus used several titles for the devil. One was 'Beelzebub, the prince of demons' (Matthew 12:24); another was 'the prince of this world' (John 14:30); and another 'the evil one' (Matthew 13:19). He also identified him as 'a murderer' and 'a liar' (John 8:44). Paul supplies us with several other titles, including 'the god of this age' (2 Corinthians 4:4), 'Belial' (2 Corinthians 6:15) – meaning 'worthlessness' – and 'the ruler of the kingdom of the air' (Ephesians 2:2); while John calls him 'the angel of the Abyss', and adds the Hebrew title 'Abaddon', with its Greek equivalent 'Apollyon' (Revelation 9:11), words which mean 'destruction'. Surely nobody can read that devastating list of names and still think of the devil in casual or light-hearted terms!

### The fall and rise of a superpower

To understand where the devil fits into the spiritual world, we need to go back beyond his names to his origin. Although some people have seen a reference to the devil's original state and subsequent history in Isaiah 14 and Ezekiel 28, it is probably safer to look elsewhere for facts about which we can be certain and there are two statements in particular which give us these. The first is where Jesus told his disciples 'I saw Satan fall like lightning from heaven' (Luke 10:18) and the second is where Paul tells Timothy that a person appointed to a position of leadership in the church 'must not be a recent convert, or he may become conceited and fall under the same judgment as the devil' (1 Timothy 3:6). From these two statements we learn that Satan must originally have been a perfect angelic being, created by God and living in heaven, but that at some stage he became 'conceited' and presumably sought to overthrow God and take over the rule of the universe. But his insane rebellion ended in disaster, and in an indescribable moment of divine judgment he was cast out of God's presence. As the Bible also speaks of 'angels who did not keep their positions of authority but abandoned their own home' (Jude 6), it would appear that an unspecified number of other angels shared his sin and were swept away at the same time. We are not given any clear information about this, but we do know that when the Bible speaks of the devil's present activities, it often links them with 'the powers of this dark world and . . . the spiritual forces of evil in the heavenly realms' (Ephesians 6:12).

It is in this sense that we can speak about the fall and rise of a superpower. Although fallen from his original heavenly status, the devil is now the head of his own satanic kingdom, an untold number of evil spirits, (sometimes called 'demons' in the Bible) whom he uses as his agents to carry out his diabolical activities. With this vast army at his disposal, he exercises tremendous power in the world, and particularly over all people who are not Christians. Paul says that 'the god of this age has blinded the minds of unbelievers, so that they cannot see the light of the gospel of the glory of Christ, who is the image of God' (2 Corinthians 4:4). He reminds the Christians at Ephesus that before their conversion, they 'followed the ways of this world and of the ruler of the kingdom of the air, the spirit who is now at work in those who are disobedient' (Ephesians 2:2). He even goes so far as to say that unconverted men are in 'the trap of the devil, who has taken them captive to do his will' (2 Timothy 2:26). Even more staggeringly, Jesus told some of his critics 'You belong to your father, the devil, and you want to carry out your father's desire' (John 8:44). The devil is not only the ruler of a kingdom, but also the head of a vast family of unconverted men and women, who gladly, even if unconsciously, carry out his wishes in their godless lives.

### Strategic warfare

But where does he feature in the Christian's life? The answer is that he is the Christian's constant, implacable opponent. Peter warns that 'Your enemy the devil prowls around like a roaring lion looking for someone to devour' (1 Peter 5:8). He is engaged, with the help of a host of unseen agents, in total warfare against every child of God, trying in every way possible to drag him into defeat, disobedience and sin. Writing to the Christians at Corinth, Paul was able to say concerning the devil 'we are not unaware of his schemes' (2 Corinthians 2:11). How many Christians can say the same thing today? Yet it is precisely here that the Bible can help us. In the modern sporting world, a professional boxer may spend hours studying films of his next opponent's previous fights. With the help of slow-motion replays, he will carefully take note of his strengths and weaknesses, his favourite punches, his methods of attack, and so on, so that when the time comes to step into the ring, he will know what to expect and how to react. For the Christian, the Bible provides an accurate record of many of the devil's previous contests, with 'action replays' of his tactics, and is therefore a tremendous help in facing up to his attacks. Here are some of the tactics we can discover.

*Firstly, the surprise attack*

King David was probably only going up to his palace roof for a breath of fresh air, but glancing around, 'he saw a woman bathing' (2 Samuel 11:2). That did it! In a moment of time, the devil had torn David apart, and eventually dragged him into a hopeless morass of dishonesty, adultery, callousness and murder. Yet it all happened so quickly! Given time to think, to weigh up the consequences, to think about an issue in the light of Christ's death on the cross, the Christian will turn aside from sin; but the sudden, stabbing attack often catches him out, and quickly leaves him beaten and ashamed. No Christian can afford to drop his guard, to be careless, to be over-confident. He must be ready to be attacked at any time and in any way.

*Secondly, the siege attack*

If the devil cannot get through with a surprise attack, he will often lay siege to the Christian's will. One of the Old Testament prophecies about the devil says that 'He will speak against the Most High and oppress his saints' (Daniel 7:25), and many Christians would sadly admit that he has sometimes done so with great success. The stone that can hardly be scratched by a sudden stab with a knife can be completely worn away by the slow, continuous dripping of water, and the Christian who seems able to cope very well with obvious and open temptation is sometimes the one who finally cracks under constant pressure. Slowly but surely, the devil convinces him that his circumstances are too difficult, that his past failures have weakened him too much, that he will just never be able to overcome some particular sin — and eventually the dam breaks. This is almost certainly what happened in the case of Judas Iscariot, the disciples' honorary treasurer. Little by little, the devil laid siege to his heart. Firstly, there would have been the growing realisation of the opportunity to make a little for himself 'on the side'. Then came the first, furtive finger in the till. Gradually, petty theft became a steady habit — John says bluntly, 'he was a thief; as keeper of the money bag, he used to help himself to what was put into it' (John 12:6). Finally, he was even prepared to betray Jesus to the authorities for 'thirty silver coins' and 'watched for an opportunity to hand him over' (Matthew 26:15—16). Check carefully that you are not letting the devil erode your standards, and that you are not being dragged down into discouragement and defeatism.

## *Thirdly, the subtle attack*

The devil is a master of disguise. The cartoonist's impression of him as ugly could scarcely be further from the truth, because the Bible says that there are times when 'Satan masquerades as an angel of light' (2 Corinthians 11:14). And if he can disguise himself in that way, he has no difficulty in making sin look innocent! The temptation of Adam and Eve in the garden of Eden is a perfect example of this. As a result of the devil's subtle insinuations, Eve saw the tree of the knowledge of good and evil not as something forbidden by God, but as 'good for food and pleasing to the eye, and also desirable for gaining wisdom' (Genesis 3:6). But what was the result? Instead of physical food, they found spiritual poison; instead of satisfaction, they found shame; instead of unlimited pleasure, they found unspeakable pain. Beware of the subtle attack! Remember that if the devil can look like an angel, he can also make vice look like virtue and error like truth. Learn to test your thoughts, opinions, desires, and assessment of suggestions and situations by the teaching of the Word of God, or you will run the risk of being caught out by the oldest tactic in the book!

## The big match

There is one particular passage in the Bible that can give us added help in studying this whole subject of the devil's methods of attack, and that is when we are told in a vivid and dramatic way of the classic encounter which took place between Jesus and Satan in the Judean wilderness. The three specific attacks that Jesus faced give us an explicit understanding of the enemy's tactics.

### *Firstly, to go before the will of God*

'If you are the Son of God', said the devil, 'tell these stones to become bread' (Matthew 4:3). Here was a clear temptation for Jesus to use his divine power in order to satisfy his bodily appetite — he had, after all, fasted for forty days and nights. But he had not received any command from his Father to do any such thing, and to Jesus his Father's word meant even more than desperately needed food. This comes out clearly in his reply. 'It is written: "Man does not live on bread alone, but on every word that comes from the mouth of God" ' (Matthew 4:4). Satan's first temptation to the first Adam was to his bodily appetite, and so was his first recorded temptation to the second Adam, and it is especially in the realm of the physical, the visible, and the immediate need, that he tempts Christians today to go before the will of God, to act first and ask questions afterwards.

### *Secondly, to go beyond the will of God*

The next temptation was quite different. Satan took

Jesus to the pinnacle of the temple in Jerusalem and said to him, 'If you are the Son of God, throw yourself down', adding with great subtly part of a quotation from Psalm 91, in which God promised that 'He will command his angels concerning you, and they will lift you up in their hands so that you will not strike your foot against a stone' (Matthew 4:5–6). But the devil's quotation from scripture was not accurate. As you will see from Psalm 91:11–12, he deliberately left out the words 'to guard you in all your ways'. The promise was not that God would protect a man regardless of how he behaved, but only when he walked along the pathway of obedience. To claim the promise of scripture in any other way would be to go beyond the will of God, and therefore to take unwarranted and unnecessary risks. Jesus quickly countered with an accurate and relevant quotation from Deuteronomy 6:16 – 'Do not put the Lord your God to the test' (Matthew 4:7). Beware of twisting the Word of God to suit your own ends! The only safe place to walk is where the Bible clearly shows the way.

### Thirdly, to go behind the will of God

The final temptation was simple, yet stunning. Showing Jesus all the kingdoms of the world, the devil told him 'All this I will give you, if you will bow down and worship me' (Matthew 4:9). The implications were enormous. The agony of the cross could be avoided if only Jesus would abandon his mission of love and worship the devil instead. But to do that would be to disobey the clear command of his Father, and Jesus replied in a flash, 'Away from me, Satan! For it is written: "Worship the Lord your God and serve him only" ' (Matthew 4:10).

There was nothing subtle or gradual about this last

temptation. It was a blatant and brutal assault upon the Saviour's will, and we can be sure that the devil will not spare us from the same kind of attack. Be ready, amongst other things, for the savage and outrageous attack! Every Christian should make a careful study of this crucial clash, and if he is to resist similar assaults, his life must be governed by this clear principle: *the will of God — nothing less, nothing more, nothing else.* We shall have a chapter on the subject of the will of God later, but for the moment notice that it is linked, as was every reply Jesus made, to the plain, unchanging teaching of the Word of God.

## Doomsday

The Bible not only outlines the devil's past, and tells us of his present activities and tactics, it also charts his future, and in doing so it tells us that he is on a collision course with ultimate judgment and condemnation. All his efforts to thwart God's purposes will eventually prove futile. Reading through the Bible, we can pick out two stages in the devil's overthrow.

### *The verdict*

The Bible says that 'The reason the Son of God appeared was to destroy the devil's work' (1 John 3:8), and that he took human nature upon him 'so that by his death he might destroy him who holds the power of death — that is, the devil — and free those who all their lives were held in slavery by their fear of death' (Hebrews 2:14—15). That sentence was openly declared when Jesus died on the cross. Jesus said, concerning his own death, 'Now is the time for judgment on this world; now the prince of this world will be driven out' (John 12:31), while Paul, using the vivid, dramatic picture of a victorious commander-in-chief stripping his defeated enemies of all their arms and insignia and dragging them behind him in a victory parade, declared that by his death Jesus 'having disarmed the powers and authorities . . . made a public spectacle of them, triumphing over them by the cross' (Colossians 2:15).

## The execution

Although, as we have seen, the devil is still able to exercise tremendous power over men, the Bible says that 'he knows that his time is short' (Revelation 12:12). His influence is limited not only by God's overruling providence, but also by the divine time-table, which promises to Christians that the day will come when God will finally 'crush Satan under your feet' (Romans 16:20). It is not strictly true to say that the devil lives in hell at the moment, but what is certain is that 'eternal fire' is 'prepared for the devil and his angels' (Matthew 25:41). In an awful moment of final judgment beyond our powers of understanding the devil and all his host will be 'thrown into the lake of burning sulphur, where the beast and the false prophet had been thrown. They will be tormented day and night for ever and ever' (Revelation 20:10). The devil's reign of terror will finally be over, and all those who have trusted Christ as their Saviour will enter into the eternal experience of what Peter means when he says that 'in keeping with (God's) promise we are looking forward to a new heaven and a new earth, the home of righteousness' (2 Peter 3:13).

## 13. TEMPTATION

Having examined something of the devil's origin,

career, tactics and future, let us now take a closer look at the question of temptation, and in order to get a clear picture of the subject we will need to begin by looking at the precise meaning of the word 'temptation' as used in the Bible.

## Testing and tempting

In some ways these two words are linked together, yet they also have an important difference. We can see this difference by putting two particular texts alongside each other. In the first we are told 'Some time later God tested Abraham . . .' (Genesis 22:1). The second reads 'When tempted, no one should say "God is tempting me". For God cannot be tempted by evil, nor does he tempt anyone' (James 1:13). Notice the difference. God told Abraham to take his only son Isaac to Mount Moriah and to offer him there as a sacrifice. Without a moment's hesitation, Abraham began to carry out these extraordinary instructions, and it was only when he had a knife poised over his son's prostrate body that God intervened and said 'Do not lay a hand on the boy. Do not do anything to him. Now I know that you fear God, because you have not withheld from me your son, your only son'. (Genesis 22:12). It was not Isaac's life that God wanted, but Abraham's faith! — and Abraham demonstrated it in the most dramatic way possible. In a nutshell, we could put it like this: God tests us in order to help us to stand, whereas the devil tempts us in order to make us fall. While all our circumstances are under God's sovereign control, and nothing can touch the Christian without God's permission, he is never directly the cause of any temptation or incitement to commit sin — and it is temptation in that sense that we are to examine in this chapter.

## The simple truth

The next thing we need to be clear about is that temptation is the common, lifelong experience of all men everywhere. Paul says 'No temptation has seized you except what is common to man' (1 Corinthians 10:13). That may sound too obvious for words, but many Christians begin to lose the battle against sin by a failure to realise this simple, basic truth. Temptation is 'common to man' — that is, to every man, the Christian as well as the non-Christian. Let us just follow this through for a moment.

*Temptation is not removed* when a person becomes a Christian. The notion that when a person comes to Christ his trials, pressures, problems and temptations are removed is totally unbiblical. It would be truer to say that as soon as a person is converted these things increase, and for the obvious reason that as soon as a person becomes a friend of God he becomes the sworn enemy of the devil.

*Temptation is not repelled* from the Christian by a life of isolation, an act of dedication, or a vow of consecration. We live in an age of instant this, capsuled that and press-button most things — but God has nowhere promised that a Christian can escape temptation by any of these methods. Nor is there a spiritual crisis or 'blessing' or 'experience' that can deliver the Christian from further attack by the devil.

*Temptation is not reduced* by a Christian's spiritual or ecclesiastical progress. No amount of victories won, knowledge gained, work done or offices held will guarantee that the devil will stand off or reduce the frequency or ferocity of his attacks.

Now it is important to grasp all of this, because it is easy to be weakened by constant temptation, to get wearied and worn by it, to get dragged into depression, to feel that somehow your constant temptation must mean that you are a failure as a Christian, and that you must have grieved God in such a way that he has deserted you. From there, it is easy to think that you might as well give up, back down, sell out. Those are the devil's lies! *Temptation is not sin, nor is it an indication of failure.* No man on earth was subject to more constant attacks from the devil than the Lord Jesus Christ. The Bible tells us that he was 'tempted in every way, just as we are — *yet was without sin'* (Hebrews 4:15). That single, superb statement should immediately put all of your temptation in its right perspective!

## War on all fronts

In modern warfare, no section of an army is more important than the Intelligence Department, which carefully monitors all the enemy's activities, and keeps its own forces fully informed of the situation on all fronts. In the Christian life, nothing is more important than that we should have a careful analysis of the areas in which the devil operates. We have already noted many of his tactics — let us now look at some of the major areas in which he uses them.

### *The moral front*

Of course all sin is immoral, but we usually think of morality in terms of the physical, the sexual — and it is in that sense that I am using it here. Sex is one of God's most precious gifts to his children, not only as a means of the reproduction of human life, but as a total expression of love and for the giving and receiving of mutual strength and comfort between married partners. Yet the devil has twisted and warped this lovely gift beyond all recognition, and used it to torment and wreck the lives of untold millions of men and women down the ages. There is no need for me to quote statistics to show the present-day decline in moral standards — they would in any event be out of date before this book reached your hands. Nor would it help to give any examples of modern outrages against common decency in the mass media of films, radio, television, and literature. Instead, let us get the basic principles of God's word firmly fixed in our minds. The Bible's standard is that 'a man will leave his father and mother and be united to his wife, and they will become one flesh' (Genesis 2:24). *That means purity before marriage.* Again, God says in the plainest possible way 'You shall not commit adultery' (Exodus 20:14). *That means purity within marriage.* Finally, the Bible says to the Christian 'Flee from sexual immorality. All other sins a man commits are outside his body, but he who sins sexually sins against his own body. Do you not know that your body is a temple of the Holy Spirit, who is in you, whom you have received from God? You are not your own; you were bought at a price. Therefore honour God with your body' (1 Corinthians 6:18—20). *That means purity outside of marriage.* Whether you are young or old, married or unmarried, be constantly on the alert for temptation along the moral front — and remember that it can be directed to the mind, the will, the desire or the imagination, as well as to the body.

## The material front

If man's physical appetite is one area in which the devil operates with great success, so is his acquisitive nature. Man is basically greedy; he wants to acquire; he has a passion to possess — and the devil knows it! Even for the maturing Christian, materialism is a great danger, and especially in the present age of subtle, sophisticated and persuasive advertising. Again, in a world of rising prices it is sometimes difficult to draw the line between a prudent concern for a reasonable living standard and an unhealthy appetite for a constantly accelerating income, and for an increasing accumulation of 'things'. Every Christian should keep a sharp lookout for danger signals in this whole area. 'Keeping up with the Joneses' might result in getting away from God!

The Bible nowhere condemns riches and material possessions as such, but it gives clear warnings that, like sex, they are dangerous and disastrous if handled wrongly. Paul warns that 'People who want to get rich fall into temptation and a trap and into many foolish and harmful desires that plunge men into ruin and destruction. For the love of money is a root of all kinds of evil. Some people, eager for money have wandered from the faith and pierced themselves with many griefs'·(1 Timothy 6:9—10). You have been warned! Get the whole question of money and material possessions in the right perspective. Remember that you are responsible to God for all the gifts that he allows you to have. And remember above all that 'what is seen is temporary, but what is unseen is eternal' (2 Corinthians 4:18).

### The mental front

This is another area in which the devil makes huge in-roads into some people's lives. When Jesus told the parable of the sower, he told of seed that fell among thorns, and likened it to people who hear the word of God, 'but as they go on their way they are choked by life's *worries,* riches and pleasures, and they do not mature' (Luke 8:14). Notice that first word! We have already thought of temptation in the areas of 'riches' and 'pleasures' — but here is a third front on which the devil attacks. Worry, doubt, tension, fear, uncertainty and anxiety are words characteristic of the age in which we live, and every Christian should be on his guard against them. The Christian who misses out on fellowship with other believers, who is satisfied with a casual daily relationship with Christ, who lets his prayer life slip away, or who is too lazy to apply himself to studying the Bible, and therefore deprives himself of his spiritual resources, will soon find that his molehills turn into mountains. Before long he will find that he begins to doubt his beliefs and to believe in his doubts, and when that happens his usefulness as a Christian shrinks almost to zero. The Bible's answer in this area is clear: 'Cast your cares on the Lord and he will sustain you; he will never let the righteous fall'. (Psalm 55:22); 'Cast all your anxiety on him because he cares for you' (1 Peter 5:7).

*The personal front*
To cover all the other areas in which the devil operates we would need to classify every sin in the book, and every way in which they can be committed. But there is one factor which has a part to play in virtually every one of them, even when it is not recognised as such — and that is *pride,* the daring exercise of spiritual independence in opposition to the revealed will of God. Unless you are a quite extraordinary person, you will have more trouble with yourself in this life than with anyone else in the whole world! If pride can take Satan from heaven to hell, it can certainly take you from your present position into a place of failure, disobedience, defeat and shame. And it is precisely because Satan knows the effects of pride so well that

he majors in this area! If you want to make progress in the Christian life, if you want to avoid barrenness, emptiness and uselessness, begin by taking time to study the Bible's teaching on the subjects of pride and humility; and pray constantly for grace to 'walk humbly with your God' (Micah 6:8). Above all, learn to act on the basis of this great promise — 'Humble yourselves before the Lord and he will lift you up' (James 4:10).

## The way to win

In the two chapters of this section, we have concentrated our thoughts largely on the character and activities of the devil, and on the methods and tactics he employs. But we can go further than that. We have already noted Paul's words that 'No temptation has seized you except what is common to man'; but he goes on to say that 'God is faithful; he will not let you be tempted beyond what you can bear. But when you are tempted he will also provide a way out, so that you can stand up under it' (1 Corinthians 10:13). In the first part of the verse we are told that there is *no escape from temptation;* in the second part we are told that there is *no excuse for sin.* By his sovereign overruling of all the devil's activities, God has promised that with every temptation will come 'a way out', divinely-ordained means for the child of God to overcome, to live a victorious Christian life. But what are these means? There is certainly no slick 'ABC of holy living' that we can tick off like a shopping list. Rather there is a biblical array of equipment available for the Christian soldier as he engages in spiritual warfare, and only constant familiarity with the items concerned, and growing confidence in their use, will enable him to employ them effectively. But what are those items? Here is a selected short-list of priority equipment:

## Item number one: vigilance

Paul says 'So then, let us not be like others who are asleep, but let us be alert and self-controlled' (1 Thessalonians 5:6). If his enemy can appear as a roaring lion one minute and as a snake in the grass the next, the Christian dare not live a slipshod, careless life.

## Item number two: prayer

Jesus tells us 'Watch and pray so that you will not fall into temptation. The spirit is willing, but the body is weak' (Matthew 26:41).

Prayer is the vital link between man's need and God's power. As the prophet Isaiah puts it, '(God) gives strength to the weary and increases the power of the weak. Even youths grow tired and weary, and young men stumble and fall; but those who hope in the Lord will renew their strength. They will soar on wings like eagles; they will run and not grow weary, they will walk and not be faint' (Isaiah 40:29–31). To face temptation without prayer is like going into a nuclear war armed with a peashooter! Learn the discipline of daily prayer, and prove the effectiveness of emergency prayer!

## Item number three: faith

John writes 'This is the victory that has overcome the world, even our faith' (1 John 5:4), while the writer to the Hebrews says that in running the race of life we are to 'fix our eyes on Jesus, the author and perfecter of our faith' (Hebrews 12:2). Even prayer will not be effective if it is just an empty form of words. When we pray, we are to have absolute faith in the nature and character of Christ, and total confidence in the promises of God. Jesus even went so far as to tell two blind men he healed 'According to your faith will it be done to you' (Matthew 9:29). By some amazing spiritual chemistry that we cannot understand, the quality of our faith affects the quality of our life, and is a crucial factor in the outcome of the temptations and testing that we face day by day. It was in the very context of temptation and sin that the disciples cried out to the Lord Jesus 'Increase our faith!' (Luke 17:5). Every Christian should do the same!

### Item number four: the full armour of God

Towards the end of his letter to the Ephesians, Paul writes 'Finally, be strong in the Lord and in his mighty power. Put on the full armour of God so that you can take your stand against the devil's schemes. For our struggle is not against flesh and blood, but against the rulers, against the authorities, against the powers of this dark world and against the spiritual forces of evil in the heavenly realms. Therefore put on the full armour of God, so that when the day of evil comes, you may be able to stand your ground, and after you have done everything, to stand. Stand firm then, with *the belt of truth* buckled around your waist, with the *breastplate of righteousness* in place, and with your feet fitted with *the gospel of peace* as a firm footing. In addition to all this, take up *the shield of faith,* with which you can extinguish all the flaming arrows of the evil one. Take the helmet of salvation and the sword of the Spirit, which is *the word of God.* And pray in the Spirit on all occasions with *all kinds of prayers and requests'* (Ephesians 6:10–18). Go over these pieces of equipment with great care; make sure you know what they mean; and use them constantly.

### Item number five: determined resistance

Of all the promises in the Bible, none is more relevant

or exhilarating just here than this one — 'Submit your-selves, then, to God. Resist the devil, and he will flee from you' (James 4:7). Here is a clear promise that whatever the temptation, the Christian can be victorious. Defeat is unnecessary. The devil *can* be made to turn and run — but only when the Christian is prepared to yield to God and to resist the devil at every point. Wholehearted obedience and wholehearted resistance are the twin success secrets here. The Apostle Paul was able to say 'I can do everything through him who gives me strength' (Philippians 4:13). Some 2,000 years later, you have the God-given privilege of saying the same thing — and of proving it in your daily life!

# Six — Following my Saviour

---

## 14. FRUITBEARING

It is always a healthy thing when a Christian stops to ask the question 'Why did God save me?' or, to expand the question a little, 'What purposes am I meant to be fulfilling as a Christian in the world?'

I am not thinking for the moment about knowing God's will in specific circumstances, but rather of the wider fulfilment of his purposes in the life of the Christian. It goes without saying that this is a fundamentally important issue, and because it is, we should expect the Bible to give clear answers to the question. It does! — and we shall look at them in two separate chapters in this section which we have entitled 'Following my Saviour'.

### By appointment to the King — fruitbearer

Of all the insignia or titles that a British company can boast in advertising its product, none is more highly cherished than the one which reads, with impressive dignity, 'By appointment to H.M. the Queen . . .'. Even the most eye-catching advertising splashed around by a rival company pales into insignificance beside that simple statement which links the company to the ruler of the land. Now the Bible teaches that every Christian carries even more impressive credentials, for Jesus told his disciples, 'You did not choose me, but I chose you to go and bear fruit — fruit that will last' (John 15:16).

A Christian is a fruitbearer, by royal and divine appointment; it is one of the solemn and sacred purposes and responsibilities of his life to 'bear fruit'.

## The master of illustration

The classic passage on the subject of fruitbearing is in John 15 and, for the purposes of this book, we can confine our study to John 15:1–8, with the addition of verse 16, which we have already quoted.

Jesus was a master of the art of illustration. What is more, he always seemed to have *le mot juste,* the right word for the right occasion, and this passage is a perfect example of what I mean. The scholars are undecided as to precisely when Jesus actually spoke these words. The previous two chapters record what happened during Jesus's last meal with his disciples, and end with the words 'Come now, let us leave' (John 14:31). Some people think that the words of John 15 were then spoken before they actually left the premises; others, that they were spoken while the group made their way through the streets of Jerusalem; and others that they were spoken further on towards the Garden of Gethsemane. The fact is that nobody knows – but it is fascinating to realise that any one of those situations would have been an ideal setting for an allegory which began 'I am the true vine and my Father is the gardener' (John 15:1). In the 'upper room' (Luke 22:12) the remains of their meal of bread and wine would have been visible on the table; in the streets of Jerusalem, they would have been within sight of the massive Herod's Temple, with its huge golden vine motif above the entrance; on the way to Gethsemane they would have passed by many small-holdings, with their carefully tended vineyards heavy with the maturing crop. In any one of those three situations the disciples would therefore have had a 'visual aid' to help drive home the simple yet profound truths Jesus taught when he spoke of bearing fruit as a picture of the Christian life.

### Fruit is not fish

In order to understand what Jesus meant by his allegory, it is obviously essential to discover the meaning of the word 'fruit'. Some people have felt that it means faithful Christian service, others that it means evangelism, or, more specifically, leading other people to Christ. Yet as we shall see throughout our whole study, none of these explanations fits the character and application of what Jesus said. Of course every Christian is under an obligation to render obedient service, as we saw in an earlier chapter, and in the same way every Christian is responsible to share in the church's ministry of evangelism, and should therefore seek to point others to Christ. But when Jesus called Peter and Andrew to leave their nets on the seashore at Lake Galilee and give themselves to the work of evangelism, he promised to make them 'fishers of men' (Matthew 4:19), not fruiterers! Fruit and fish are not the same, and successful evangelism does not fit naturally as an explanation of what Jesus meant by 'fruit' in this passage. Then what does 'fruit' mean? Beyond any doubt, the most obvious and natural explanation is that it means what Paul describes as 'the fruit of the Spirit', that is, 'love, joy, peace, patience, kindness, goodness, faithfulness, gentleness and self-control' (Galatians 5:22—23). In other words to bear fruit is to exhibit in one's daily life those spiritual qualities that are the natural result of the Holy Spirit's indwelling and that reflect the character of the Lord Jesus himself. That certainly fits in with the Bible's consistent teaching as to the purpose of a Christian's salvation. As Paul says so clearly, 'For those God foreknew he also predestined to be conformed to the likeness of his Son' (Romans 8:29). To put it in its simplest possible form, spiritual fruitbearing means becoming more and more like Jesus, by the power of the Holy Spirit.

### The dreadful danger

The 'fruitbearing' passage in John 15 contains one of the most serious warnings in the whole Bible. After explaining that he was the true vine and his Father the gardener, Jesus went on to say 'He cuts off every branch in me that bears no fruit . . .' (v.2), adding later 'If anyone does not remain in me, he is like a branch that is thrown away and withers; such branches are picked up, thrown into the fire, and burned' (v.6). There can be no doubt as to what Jesus meant by that last phrase. In an earlier parable in which he described Christians as 'wheat' and unbelievers as 'weeds', he said that the day would come when God, the divine farmer, would order his reapers to 'collect the weeds and tie them in bundles to be burned' (Matthew 13:30). Later, he warned of a day of judgment when he would dismiss all unbelievers from his presence with the words 'Depart from me, you who are cursed, into the eternal fire prepared for the devil and his angels' (Matthew 25:41). The language in those passages is so similar to that used in John 15 that we can certainly take it that they all refer to the same thing — eternal separation from God's presence. When Jesus talks of branches being cut off and cast out he is saying no less than that they are doomed to eternal damnation.

But who are these doomed branches? Is there any suggestion here that it is possible to become a Christian and then to sin in such a way that you will be cut off, cast out, and eternally lost? Certainly not! That would contradict the Bible's clear and consistent teaching on the subject, including the words of Jesus himself, who using another simile for Christians, said 'My sheep listen to my voice; I know them, and they follow me. I give them eternal life, and they shall never perish; no one can snatch them out of my hand. My Father, who has given them to me, is greater than all, no one can snatch them out of my Father's hand' (John 10:27—29). If there was not another passage on the subject in the whole Bible, those words alone would be sufficient to prove that no Christian can ever lose his eternal salvation.

### No grapes from thorns; no figs from thistles

The clue to the identity of the doomed branches is in two phrases in John 15. In verse 2, we are told that the branch 'bears no fruit', and in verse 6 Jesus speaks of the man who 'does not remain in me', and the more closely you examine them the clearer the truth becomes. A fruitless person is not a *failed* Christian, but a *false* one — in other words, not a Christian at all! The person who professes to be a Christian, but subsequently produces none of the fruit of the Spirit in his life, is either consciously or unconsciously a liar. Conversion means change; if there has been no change in a person's life, there has been no conversion — and an unconverted person can never be said to 'remain' in Christ. Jesus himself put this so plainly in the course of the Sermon on the Mount, when he warned of people who would make false claims about themselves. His teaching there is such a perfect commentary on the phrases we are studying at the moment, that we can virtually let it speak for itself. 'Watch out for false prophets', said Jesus, 'They come to you in sheep's clothing, but inwardly they are ferocious wolves. By their fruit you will recognise them. Do people pick grapes from thorn bushes, or figs from thistles? Likewise every good tree bears good fruit, but a bad tree bears bad fruit. A good tree cannot bear bad fruit, and a bad tree cannot bear good fruit. Every tree that does not bear good fruit is cut down and thrown into the fire. Thus, *by their fruit you will recognise them'* (Matthew 7:15—20). Notice the words I have emphasised! We are entitled to judge the reality of a man's faith by the quality of his life; and if a man bears no fruit whatever, we can draw the conclusion that he is not in vital union with Jesus, the true vine, whatever claims he might make for himself.

### Remember Judas

In the face of such a solemn warning, it must have been a great comfort to the eleven disciples to hear Jesus tell them 'You are already clean because of the word I have spoken to you' (John 15:3). They would have remembered that earlier the same evening, while they had been sitting at the meal table, Jesus had said virtually the same thing with one important difference. On that occasion, he said 'You are clean, *though not every one of you'*, John adding the explanation 'For he knew who was going to betray him and that was why he said not every one was clean' (John 13:10—11). Gathered around the true vine there were eleven genuine branches and one false one, Judas Iscariot. To all outward appearances he was a Christian. He met with the others; he spoke their language; he was just as active; he was even, as we saw in an earlier chapter, the treasurer of the group. Nor is there any reason to doubt that he shared in the remarkable miracles that the disciples found themselves able to perform. But the tragedy of Judas was that all his connections were outward. He had no vital, personal, spiritual link with Christ. He caught fish, but he did not bear fruit! Every professing Christian should learn that lesson well! Paul warns the Corinthians – and us – 'Examine yourselves to see whether you are in the faith; test yourselves. Do you not realise that Christ Jesus is in you – unless, of course, you fail the test?' (2 Corinthians 13:5). It is the life that matters, not the label! Only the natural production of spiritual fruit will do as evidence that you are a genuine branch of the true vine. Remember Judas! And at the same time remember that outward attachment to the church, by baptism, attendance, membership or service, is neither the fruit required nor the means of producing it. As Jesus himself put it, 'I am the vine; you are the branches. If a man remains in me and I in him he will bear much fruit; apart from me you can do nothing (John 15:3).

### Pruning for a purpose

Continuing with his picture of the Christian as the branch of the vine, and God as the vinedresser, Jesus now adds another tremendously challenging truth. Having stated that every branch bearing no fruit is taken away, he says 'every branch that does bear fruit he trims clean so that it will be even more fruitful' (v.2). Pruning, of course, is a matter of elementary horticulture. When the branches of a tree produce too vigorous growth, or are in danger of running to wood, the wise gardener trims them, cuts them back, in order that the bursting energy rising from the parent tree might be channelled into fruit, and not just into foliage or flower. It is this picture that Jesus is using here, but with an even deeper meaning. Trimming involves not only the cutting away of rank growth, but also the removal of fungus, parasites, and foreign matter of any kind that would endanger the production of a healthy crop.

Jesus now takes that kind of picture and applies it to the life of the Christian. As we have already seen, God's great purpose for the Christian here on earth is that he should 'bear fruit' (v.16), and just as a wise gardener will tend his vines with great care in order to produce a better crop, so the heavenly vinedresser is constantly at work so that the branches of his spiritual vine will become increasingly fruitful. If you are a Christian, you should rejoice at this! *God is at work in your life!* — and his whole object is that you should be 'even more fruitful'. But what does he use as a pruning-knife, and as a means to cleanse away hindrances to fruitfulness? We could put the answer to that question in two phrases — his sovereign will and his sanctifying word.

### *Firstly, his sovereign will*

There is no greater truth in the whole Bible than that God 'does as he pleases with the powers of heaven and the peoples of the earth. No one can hold back his hand or say to him: "What have you done?" ' (Daniel 4:35). Notice those words 'as he pleases'! A human gardener may do what he pleases in a certain situation, only to discover that he has made a mistake, and ruined his crop as a result. But the heavenly vinedresser is the one of whom the Bible says 'Great is our Lord, and mighty in power; his understanding has no limit' (Psalm 147:5). This means that when he does 'what he pleases' he is doing what is best! David says 'As for God, his way is perfect' (Psalm 18:30), while Paul speaks of God's will as being 'good, pleasing and perfect'

(Romans 12:2). Here is a great truth for the Christian to grasp. God's dealings with your life may seem strange at times. You may feel that if God is moving at all, he is moving in mysterious ways. You may not be able to understand why certain things have happened, why certain problems have arisen, why something has gone wrong, why a particular pleasure has turned sour, why the sky has turned dark and the road become rough. When you feel like that, remember this: God is in sovereign control of every circumstance of your life, and will never allow anything to come into it that is not designed in his over-ruling providence to be used as a means of bringing blessing to you and glory to him! It may cut like a pruning-knife, but it will always be with a view to greater fruitfulness.

Some years ago, I was asked to write a magazine article in a series entitled 'My Text'. I could have chosen any one of hundreds, but eventually settled on these words from the Old Testament — 'For the Lord God is a sun and shield; the Lord bestows favour and honour; *no good thing does he withhold from those whose walk is blameless'* (Psalm 84:11). To live with that conviction is to be delivered from faithless anxiety and unwarranted fear — but it does mean allowing the Lord to decide what is or is not a 'good thing' as far as you are concerned! The Lord is not under any obligation to give *reasons* for his dealings with you, but he does want to *see results!* — and those results are the increasing fruitfulness of which Jesus speaks. To understand this vital truth is to make it so much easier to come to terms with the teaching of the Apostle James — 'Consider it pure joy, my brothers, whenever you face trials of many kinds, because you know that the testing of your faith develops perseverance. Perseverance must finish its work so that you may be mature and complete, not lacking anything' (James 1:2–4). The sovereign will of God is designed to produce mature and fruitful Christians.

## Secondly, his sanctifying word

We can be sure that this is one of the means God employs, for Jesus specifically goes on to say 'You are already clean because of the word I have spoken to you' (John 13:10). This ties in exactly with his prayer on behalf of all Christians, 'Sanctify them by the truth; your word is truth' (John 17:17). When the Bible is read, studied, understood and obeyed, it always has a cleansing effect. Its statements about God, man and their relationship to each other cleanse us from ignorance and error; its warnings are meant to keep us clear of sin, harm and danger; its promises are intended to keep us from empty, useless living. We shall devote a chapter to the Bible later, but for the moment let us be quite clear about this: only the Christian who is prepared to apply himself to the Word of God, and submit himself unreservedly to its teaching, is ever going to be filled with 'the knowledge of his will through all spiritual wisdom and understanding' and 'live a life worthy of the Lord . . . bearing fruit in every good work' and 'growing in the knowledge of God' (Colossians 1:9–10).

## Remain! Remain! Remain!

In all of this great teaching about fruitbearing, the word 'remain' dominates the whole passage, and all the doctrinal truth which centres around the word is brought to a practical head in the only commandment in the first eight verses — 'Remain in me' (v.4). We can get something of the meaning of the word 'remain' by noting that the original Greek word *meno,* is also translated 'continue', 'dwell', 'endure', 'abide' and 'tarry' in various English versions of the Bible. It is virtually impossible to capture the full implications of the word in its context here, but if we had to paraphrase it, we could say that it means something like 'make yourself at home'! To abide in Christ is to make him the centre of your thoughts, your plans, your hopes, and your ambitions. It is to submit your mind to his mind, your will to his will, your heart to his heart. It is to die daily to self, and to live as Paul said he did when he wrote to the Galatians, 'I have been crucified with Christ and I no longer live, but Christ lives in me. The life I live in the body, I live by faith in the Son of God, who loved me and gave himself for me' (Galatians 2:20). And when a man lives like that, Jesus promises that at least three things will follow.

*Firstly,* 'I will remain in you' (v.4). This brings out the element of promise. When a Christian gives himself wholly to the Lord, the Lord will give himself wholly to the Christian. Fulness of devotion will bring fulness of blessing.

*Secondly,* 'If you remain in me, and my words remain in you, ask whatever you wish and it will be given you' (v.7). The more a Christian abides in Christ the more he grows in grace. The more he grows in grace, the more he will pray according to the will of God. And the more he prays according to God's will, the more he will know the joy of answered prayer. The Christian's prayer life is not contained in a water-tight compartment. It is crucially affected by his whole spiritual condition.

*Thirdly,* 'This is to my Father's glory, that you bear much fruit, showing yourselves to be my disciples' (v.8). Jesus had linked these last two promises earlier, when he said 'I will do whatever you ask in my name, so that the Son may bring glory to the Father. You may ask me for anything in my name, and I will do it' (John 14:13–14) – and it is easy to see why they are linked. The Christian who is abiding in Christ, experiencing the fulness of God's blessing in his life, praying according to God's will, and knowing the joy of answered prayer, will be reproducing the life of Christ, and therefore bringing glory to God's name by fulfilling his purposes. Or, to end with Christ's own illustration, every characteristic of a grape suggests the vine from which it comes. The colour, shape, taste, flesh and perfume of a grape are unique, distinctive and eloquent. They speak of the vine. And the Christian who lives in such a way that his character speaks of Christ is one who is bringing glory to the name of his heavenly Father.

## 15. WITNESSING

We have looked at the first of two answers to the question 'What purposes am I meant to be fulfilling as a Christian in the world?', and we saw from the early part of John 15 that a Christian is expected to abide in Christ, bearing an abundance of spiritual fruit, to the glory of God. The second answer to the question comes later in the same chapter, where Jesus, promising the Holy Spirit to his disciples, says 'When the Counsellor comes, whom I will send to you from the Father, the Spirit of truth, who goes out from the Father, he will testify about me; *but you also must testify,* for you have been with me from the beginning' (John 15:26–27). The Christian is not only called to bear fruit, but to bear witness!

## Called in and sent out

Early in the gospel narrative, we read that Jesus 'went up into the hills and called to him those he wanted – designating them apostles – that they might be with him and that he might send them out to preach' (Mark 3:13–14). That last sentence neatly and accurately links this chapter with the last. Those early disciples were first called by Jesus to be 'with him', and then sent out to share with the world the good news of salvation. In other words, they were to abide and to serve, to worship and to witness. They were called in and sent out – and so is every Christian in the world today.

## The eye-witnesses

For many years I worked in and around the Law Courts in the Channel Island of Guernsey, but even if I had not had that background, I would have known one fundamental truth about witnesses: they must be people with first-hand experience of the subject on which they speak. The man who begins by saying that he understands that a friend of a neighbour of his was told something or other will soon be dismissed by the judge! A witness need not be highly intelligent, widely read, impressive in appearance, or eloquent in speech – but it is essential that he gives a personal, first-hand account of his experience. It is interesting to see how clearly this comes across in the New Testament. With an obvious reference to what happened when he, James and John saw Jesus transfigured on the mountain-top (as recorded in Mark 9), Peter writes 'We did not follow cleverly invented stories when we told you about the power and coming of our Lord Jesus Christ, but we were eye-witnesses of his majesty' (2 Peter 1:16), while in an earlier letter he calls himself 'a witness of Christ's sufferings' (1 Peter 5:1). John begins the first of his letters in the same impressive way — 'That which was from the beginning, which we have heard, which we have seen with our eyes, which we have looked at and our hands have touched — this we proclaim concerning the Word of life. The life appeared; we have seen it and testify to it, and we proclaim to you the eternal life, which was with the Father and has appeared to us. We proclaim to you what we have seen and heard, so that you also may have fellowship with us' (1 John 1:1–3). And the meaning of what they saw in the flesh, every Christian has since seen by faith! You have been to the cross, and seen yourself as a guilty sinner. You have seen God's amazing love in providing such a way of salvation. You have seen his justice satisfied in the death of his Son, and your debt paid by his sacrifice. As an eye-witness, you have a God-given duty to testify!

### God's gossips

It is one of the greatest tragedies in the church today that so many Christians are reluctant to witness for Christ, and it is an added tragedy that they can find so many excuses for not doing so. One of the commonest is 'I am not very good at that sort of thing. I think we should leave it to the professional preachers, or to those especially called to teach in the church'. But that is certainly not the picture we have in the New Testament, as we can see from one illuminating incident. Luke tells us that in the early days of the church 'a great persecution broke out against the church at Jerusalem, and all *except the apostles* were scattered throughout Judea and Samaria . . . Those who had been scattered preached the word wherever they went' (Acts 8:1,4). The important thing to notice is that the apostles, the 'professionals', remained in Jerusalem; it was the other Christians, the rank and file members of the church, who were scattered all over the land, *and who preached the gospel wherever they went.* Historians are agreed that one of the greatest reasons for the success of the early church was the way in which 'ordinary' Christians shared the good news of their faith with other people on a personal basis. While it is true that there is no substitute for the public preaching of the gospel, and while it is equally true that today's modern media of radio, television and the printed page have brought about a revolution in the speed at which millions can now be reached, it is also true that there is no escaping our personal responsibility to share the gospel with others. It is at this level that some of the most effective, penetrating and lasting evangelistic impact is made. Never be ashamed or afraid to 'gossip the gospel'; you will be surprised how often God gives you the right word for the right person at the right time.

## The word of truth

Other Christians who are reluctant to speak to others about their faith make the excuse, 'I tend to be a *practical* person, and I feel that the most important thing is to let my life speak'. Now that is a very subtle half-truth! Of course it *is* important that the quality of our lives should be such that people will be made to think, and we have carefully studied the importance of godly living in the chapters on sanctification and fruitbearing. That is exactly the kind of thing Jesus meant when he said 'let your light shine before men, that they may see your good deeds and praise your Father in heaven' (Matthew 5:16). *But that is not enough.* The Bible teaches that a Christian is not only to be a person of good works, but of good words! Let me illustrate. A friend of yours suffering from a severe rash on his skin tries all kinds of treatment without success. When you meet him you notice that his complaint is identical to one from which you had suffered some years before, but which had been completely cured by the application of a particular ointment. Now it would be no help to your friend for you to show him that your hands and arms were completely free of blemish; what he would need was the name of the ointment. Your 'good works' (the clear texture of your skin), would need to be followed by 'good words' (information as to how it was achieved). Paul tells the Ephesians 'And you also were included in Christ *when you heard the word of truth,* the gospel of your salvation' (Ephesians 1:13). Writing to the Romans, he repeats Joel's marvellous prophecy that 'Everyone who calls on the name of the Lord will be saved', but immediately adds these penetrating questions – 'How, then, can they call on the one they have not believed in?. And how can they believe in the one of whom they have not heard? And how can they hear without someone preaching to them? And how can they preach unless they are sent?' (Romans 10:13–15). And to clinch the whole point, he adds a verse or two later *'faith comes from hearing the message,* and the message is heard through the word of Christ' (Romans 10:17). In genuine Christian witness, works and words are not alternatives, they are partners. It is not enough for a Christian to show his salvation; he should also be prepared to speak about it.

### Not only what but who

When Paul wrote about 'the word of truth, the gospel

of your salvation' his choice of language was perfect. The Bible *is* 'the word of truth'. It tells us the truth about God, man, sin, heaven, hell, faith, holiness, and about every other subject on which it speaks. And essentially it is 'the gospel of your salvation; the good news that even the worst of sinners can get right with God. But as Paul himself points out so clearly, God's good news is 'the gospel . . . *regarding his Son*' (Romans 1:2—3), 'the gospel of *His Son*' (Romans 1: 9). The gospel is not based on philosophy, but on history; not on ideas, but on events; and those events centre on the Lord Jesus Christ. The purpose of evangelism is not to indoctrinate people with propositions, but to introduce them to a person! Now in the course of discussion with an unbeliever you may well find yourself talking about a wide variety of issues, but always remember that at the end of the day what really matters is that you introduce the sinner to the Saviour. When Andrew met the Lord he immediately went to his brother and 'brought Simon to Jesus' (John 1:42). When Nathaniel questioned whether Jesus was really the Messiah, Philip simply invited him to 'Come and see' (John 1:46). Later, when he had the opportunity of speaking to a high-ranking Ethiopian politician who was reading the Old Testament in a search for the truth, Philip the evangelist 'began with that very passage of Scripture and told him *the good news about Jesus*' (Acts 8:35).

The story is told of two ferry boats passing each other on the Mississippi River. An old coloured workman leaning on the rail of one of them pointed to the other boat and said to the passenger beside him 'Look, there's the captain'. 'Yes', replied the passenger, 'but why do you mention him?' 'Years ago', said the workman, 'that man rescued me when I fell overboard, and ever since then I just loves to point him out!' Surely a Christian should be happy to point out the one who rescued him from sin!

## Who wants to be a martyr!

The New Testament word 'witness' translates the original Greek word *martur,* from which we get our English word martyr. This is a necessary reminder to us that consistent Christian living and faithful Christian witness is difficult and costly. For untold thousands of Christians, from New Testament times onwards, it has meant the laying down of their lives, and far from being a thing of the past, it has been said that more Christians have been killed for their faith in the 20th Century than in any previous century in the church's history, mainly, of course, at the hands of Nazis and Communists. Many other Christians today, especially in Eastern Europe, are in slave camps or prisons. Others are cut off from their families, or socially suppressed, or prevented from holding certain positions, or deprived of advanced education, solely because of their Christian commitment. These, too, are martyrs, and should find a constant place in our prayers. Yet the Bible makes it clear that whole-hearted Christian living and witness will always be costly in one way or another. Paul, for instance, says that 'everyone who wants to live a godly life in Christ Jesus will be persecuted' (2 Timothy 3:12). And Jesus himself, in the context of the verses with which we began this chapter, explains why this is so — 'If the world hates you, keep in mind that it hated me first. If you belonged to the world, it would love you as its own. As it is, you do not belong to the world, but I have chosen you out of the world. That is why the world hates you. Remember the words I spoke to you:

"No servant is greater than his master". If they persecuted me they will persecute you. If they obeyed my teaching, they will obey yours also' (John 15:18– 20). Every Christian should study that statement very carefully! There is of course no suggestion here that every Christian is hated and persecuted by every non-Christian at every moment of his life, but it does explain why as a Christian you face difficulties when you seek to live purely and witness faithfully. It is because 'you do not belong to the world'. At your conversion, you were 'rescued from the dominion of darkness and brought ... into the kingdom of the Son (God) loves' (Colossians 1:13), with the immediate result that the devil began to deploy his spiritual agents against you. The devil attacks in a thousand different ways, and when you seek to witness, the devil brings opposition, or criticism, or misunderstanding, or embarrassment, or fear of ridicule, or any one of a multitude of other things to bear upon you, in a deliberate attempt to shut your mouth and depress your spirit. And far too often his tactics pay off. You begin to think that perhaps spiritual subjects are too deep to raise with certain friends, or that you might give offence, or that you might appear self-righteous. Or, to be honest, you may be just plain afraid of being thought some kind of religious freak; as the old writer put it, 'Fear of man will prove to be a snare' (Proverbs 29:25).

What should be your answer to all this? Begin by recognising the reality of the situation. Settle for the fact that in seeking to witness you are working, as it were, behind enemy lines. Realise that there are times when you will have to pay the price of being a Christian 'martyr'. And remember the promise Jesus made when he said 'Blessed are you when people insult you, persecute you and falsely say all kinds of evil against you because of me. Rejoice and be glad, because *great is your reward in heaven,* for in the same way they persecuted the prophets who were before you' (Matthew 5:11–12).

## The vital witness

In a court of law, there is sometimes a key witness whose evidence turns the whole course of a case. His words carry such weight with the judge and jury that they constitute the decisive factor in the outcome of the proceedings. In Christian things there is also a vital witness, whose influence is even more decisive – the Holy Spirit! Notice how perfectly Jesus times the appearance of this key witness on the pages of the New Testament! It was immediately after warning the disciples of the hatred and opposition they would face, that Jesus added the words quoted at the beginning of this chapter – 'When the Counsellor comes, whom I will send to you from the Father, the Spirit of truth who goes out from the Father, *he will testify about me;* but you also must testify, for you have been with me from the beginning' (John 15:26–27). This is perhaps the most important verse on the subject of witnessing in the whole of the New Testament. Left to themselves, Christians would never succeed in being effective witnesses. No amount of eloquence, persuasion or argument will ever convince a single person of the truth of the Christian faith. The only reason why a Christian can ever 'win a case' is because the Holy Spirit's voice has carried decisive weight. Jesus promised those early disciples that the Holy Spirit would 'convict the world of guilt in regard to sin and righteousness and judgment' (John 16:8). Now while it is true that most people in the world reject the witness of the Holy Spirit, just as most rejected Jesus when they heard him in the flesh, it is also true that every day, in every corner of the world, his decisive voice is breaking through into the hearts and minds of unbelievers, enabling them to understand the truth about God, persuading them to admit their own condition and need, and drawing them to repentance and faith, so that the day will come when we shall see the fulfilment of John's prophecy of 'a great multitude that no one could count, from every nation, tribe, people and language, standing before the throne and in front of the Lamb' (Revelation 7:9). That should be a tremendous encouragement to you as a Christian and as a witness for Christ! The work of Christ and the witness of the Spirit will not end in failure or disappointment, but in the glorious triumph of the salvation of all those who were chosen in Christ before the foundation of the world. To share in the trials of evangelism here and now will be to share in its triumph there and then. No Christian could possibly have a greater incentive to witness for Christ!

# Seven — Doing my duty

## 16. THE HOLY SPIRIT

Perhaps no issue in Christianity causes so much confusion and difference of opinion as the doctrine of the Holy Spirit. What or who is the Holy Spirit? If he is a person, what is his nature and character? What is his relationship to the Christian? What does he do? What is meant by being baptised with the Spirit? How can a Christian be filled with the Spirit? What about the gifts of the Spirit? The questions are endless, and the arguments sometimes conducted in a way sadly different from the attitude of the Lord Jesus, who was 'full of grace and truth' (John 1:14). In a book of this size, we will only be able to outline some areas of the subject, but we shall do so with one clear guideline — 'What does the Scripture say?' (Romans 4:3). Only by keeping firmly to the Bible's own teaching will we avoid the extravagances, excesses and eccentricities that have caused confusion and distress in the lives of so many people.

### A person, not a thing

The first issue to be settled is that the Holy Spirit is a living person. He is not merely a quality, an influence, or a power. Some people speak of the Holy Spirit coming into the life of the church as if they were discussing having electricity laid on or central heating put in, but that sort of language is nothing short of blasphemous. In the Bible, we read of the Holy Spirit speaking to people, striving with others, sending others into a particular sphere of Christian service; activities that could never be attributed to a mere quality, influence or power. Yet we can settle the question of the Holy Spirit's nature by looking at just one sentence spoken by Jesus. Shortly before his death, he promised his disciples that after his resurrection and ascension the Holy Spirit would come to them, and he then went on to say, 'But when he, the Spirit of truth, comes, he will guide you into all truth. He will not speak on his own; he will speak only what he hears, and he will tell you what is yet to come' (John 16:13). Notice that the words 'he' and 'his' occur no less than seven times in that one verse — impressive proof of the living personality of the Holy Spirit.

## One of three

The second fact to settle in our minds is that the Holy Spirit is not merely a person, but a divine person. *He is God,* and not merely a supernatural being who acts on God's behalf. This can be proved in so many ways: here are three of them.

*Firstly, statements made by God in the Old Testament are said in the New Testament to have been made by the Holy Spirit.*

To give just one example, God's words to the prophet in Isaiah 6:9—10 are quoted by the Apostle Paul with the introduction 'The Holy Spirit spoke the truth to your forefathers when he said through Isaiah the prophet . . .' (Acts 28:25).

*Secondly, qualities which clearly belong only to God are attributed to the Holy Spirit.*

He is present everywhere: David asks 'Where can I go

from your Spirit? Where can I flee from your presence?'
(Psalm 139:7). He is possessed of total knowledge:
Paul says that 'the Spirit searches all things, even the
deep things of God' (1 Corinthians 2:10). He has divine
power: when Mary asked how she could give birth to
the promised Messiah without having a husband, the
angel told her 'The Holy Spirit will come upon you,
and the power of the Most High will overshadow you.
So the holy one to be born will be called the Son of
God' (Luke 1:35).

*Thirdly, sinning against the Holy Spirit is said to be
sinning against God.*

At a time when the early Christians agreed to sell up
their property and pool the proceeds, a man called
Ananias and his wife Sapphira dishonestly kept back
some money for themselves. Rebuking them, the
Apostle Peter said 'Ananias, how is it that Satan has
so filled your heart that you have lied to the Holy
Spirit and have kept for yourself some of the money
you received for the land? . . . You have not lied to
men but to God' (Acts 5:3—4).

These three instances alone are sufficient proof of
the deity of the Holy Spirit, but to accept that truth
immediately raises the issue of the Holy Trinity, the
doctrine that while God is essentially one, he is one in
three distinct persons, the Father, the Son and the Holy
Spirit. The word 'Trinity' does not actually occur in the
Bible, and the original equivalent of the word was not
used until the 2nd Century, but it is an excellent way
of crystallising the Bible's teaching that God is a 'tri-
unity', one God but three persons. No theologian in the
history of the world has ever been able to *explain* the
doctrine of the Trinity, because it is beyond human
reason. The simplest possible thing we can do is to
accept the plain teaching of the Bible, which we can

sum up in these six straightforward statements: The Father is God. The Son is God. The Holy Spirit is God. The Father is not the Son. The Son is not the Holy Spirit. The Holy Spirit is not the Father. While God is one in essence and nature, each of the three persons in the godhead is distinctly and equally divine. The Holy Spirit is not, therefore, one of three gods, but one of three persons in the eternal godhead. Again, while Christians think of him as the third person of the Trinity, this in no way means that he is inferior to the Father or the Son. It is, however, a natural way of expressing the order in which the personalities of the members of the godhead are revealed in the Bible. To sum up, the Holy Spirit is God — sovereign, eternal, and divine — and is therefore to be worshipped, glorified, honoured and obeyed.

## Nothing without the spirit

In the course of his talk on fruitbearing, which we studied in an earlier chapter, Jesus told his disciples 'apart from me you can do nothing' (John 15:5). It is interesting (and another indication of their equality) to notice that that statement would also be true if spoken by the Holy Spirit, because without his work in our hearts and lives we would have no sense of God, no means of coming to know him, and no power to obey him. We can follow this through by going back over the previous six sections in this book, and noting how essential is the work of the Holy Spirit in each area we have studied so far. Nor need there be an apology for repetition: when Peter was writing about basic facts of the Christian faith he said 'I will always remind you of these things, even though you know them and are firmly established in the truth you now have' (2 Peter 1:12). The first section was *Why do I need God?* and it dealt with sin and guilt. While all men need God, not all men realise the fact; and while all men are guilty sinners, not all men are conscious of their condition. The Bible says that it is the Holy Spirit alone who can 'convict the world of guilt in regard to sin and righteousness and judgment' (John 16:8). Without the work of the Holy Spirit, a man will never have a clear consciousness of his spiritual condition and need.

The second section was *How can I find God?* and it dealt with the new birth, repentance and faith. When Jesus told Nicodemus 'Unless a man is born again, he cannot see the kingdom of God' (John 3:3), he added 'Unless a man is born of water *and the Spirit,* he cannot enter the kingdom of God' (John 3:5). It is the Holy Spirit who brings about the miracle of the new birth and leads a man to repentance and faith. That means that nobody can become a Christian without receiving the Holy Spirit; there is no other way into the kingdom of God. But another important truth flows from this, and we ought to take a moment to emphasise it at this point, and that is that *every Christian has received the Holy Spirit.* Paul reminds the Galatian believers that their first steps in the Christian life were 'beginning with the Spirit' (Galatians 3:3), and he tells the Romans quite clearly that 'if anyone does not have the Spirit of Christ, he does not belong to Christ' (Romans 8:9). A Christian may not always be conscious of the Holy Spirit's *presence,* but he would not even *be* a Christian in his *absence!* It is the Holy Spirit who brings the dead soul of life, and who introduces a person into the kingdom of God, and into the Christian Church. The Bible says 'We were all baptised by one Spirit into one body — whether Jews or Greeks, slave or free — and we were all given the one Spirit to drink' (1 Corinthians 12:13). When a person finds God, is born again, becomes a Christian, is placed into the Christian Church, which the Bible calls the body of Christ, it is all said to be the work of the Holy Spirit.

The third section was *What does God offer me?* In it we studied the great Christian doctrines of justification, adoption and assurance, and in each of these we saw that the work of the Holy Spirit was absolutely vital. It is interesting to notice how this is brought out in one New Testament chapter. With regard to justification, we discovered that this is possible only because of the death and resurrection of Christ on behalf of his people — and Paul tells the Romans that 'the Spirit of him who raised Jesus from the dead is living in you' (Romans 8:11). With regard to adoption, we saw that this was the specific work of the Holy Spirit, and that one of his titles is 'the Spirit of sonship' (Romans 8:15). With regard to assurance, that settled conviction of heart and mind that we are Christians, the Bible tells us that in this area 'the Spirit himself testifies with our spirit that we are God's children' (Romans 8:16). In a nutshell, then, the Holy Spirit makes real to the Christian all that the Father determined to give and all that the Son died to bring.

The fourth section was *Pleasing my Father,* and in it we looked at the subjects of sanctification, service and watchfulness. The last of these three is really caught up in the other two — to be biblically watchful is to be living and working in ways that are pleasing to the Lord. And how can we do that? — only by the enabling of the Holy Spirit. As far as sanctification, our gradual growth in holiness, is concerned, Paul says that we are 'being transformed into (the Lord's) likeness with ever increasing glory' and immediately adds that this glory 'comes from the Lord who is the Spirit' (2 Corinthians

3:18). As far as our Christian service is concerned, God tells us that this will be effective 'Not by might, nor by power but by my spirit' (Zechariah 4:6). Only the Holy Spirit can enable the Christian to live and work in a way that will please the Father.

The fifth section was *Fighting my enemy,* when we studied the person and work of Satan and the whole question of temptation. Having done so, we need hardly take much time here to prove that if we are going to be successful in the fight against temptation and sin we need nothing less than to be strengthened 'with power through (God's) Spirit' (Ephesians 3:16).

The sixth section was *Following my Saviour,* and in it we looked at the questions of fruitbearing and witnessing. But the fruit we are called upon to bear is described in the New Testament as 'the fruit of the Spirit' (Galatians 5:22), and Christ's declaration to his disciples that they would be his witnesses all over the world only came after the words 'But you will receive power when the Holy Spirit comes on you' (Acts 1:8). As in all the other sections we studied, the presence and power of the Holy Spirit in the Christian's heart is absolutely essential for his spiritual life, health and effectiveness.

## The gifts

We began this chapter by saying that there was a great deal of confusion in the church today about the doctrine of the Holy Spirit, and it would probably be true to add that much of it touches at some point on the question of what are called 'the gifts of the Spirit'. Many Christians are led to believe that in order to fulfil God's purpose for their lives they should be seeking for some dramatic encounter with the Holy Spirit which will result in them receiving one or more exciting spiritual gifts, such as the ability to speak with 'tongues' and that this new experience and these exciting gifts will at one and the same time be the essence and the evidence of God's special blessing on their lives. Now this is a very controversial issue, and we will by no means be able to explore the subject at any length in a book of this size, but we must certainly take time to lay down some clear biblical principles in this area. Let us begin by reading carefully through the two key New Testament passages on the subject. Firstly, Paul tells the Corinthians 'There are different kinds of gifts, but the same Spirit. There are different kinds of service, but the same Lord. There are different kinds of working, but the same God works all of them in all men. Now to each one the manifestation of the Spirit is given for the common good. To one there is given through the Spirit the message of wisdom, to another the message of knowledge by means of the same Spirit, to another faith by the same Spirit, to another gifts of healing by that one Spirit, to another miraculous powers, to another prophecy, to another the ability to distinguish between spirits, to another the ability to speak in different kinds of tongues, and to still another the interpretation of tongues. All these are the work of one and the same Spirit, and he gives them to each man, just as he determines.' (1 Corinthians 12:4–11). The second passage is in Paul's letter to the Romans, and reads 'We have different gifts, according to the grace given us. If a man's gift is prophesying, let him use it in proportion to his faith. If it is serving, let him serve; if it is teaching, let him teach; if it is encouraging, let him encourage; if it is contributing to the needs of others, let him give generously; if it is leadership, let him govern diligently; if it is showing mercy, let him do it cheerfully'

(Romans 12:6–8). Now what are the principles we can establish from these two passages?

### *Firstly, not all the gifts of the Spirit are exotic or sensational*

Things like prophecy, the working of miracles and speaking in tongues might well cause excited comment, but notice that serving, teaching, giving and works of mercy are also included in the list! It is dangerously wrong to limit the gifts of the Spirit to those likely to, attract excited attention. When the early church chose out seven men 'full of the Spirit and wisdom' (Acts 6:3), it was not in order to perform some sensational ministry, but to administer the non-contributory pensions being paid to certain Greek widows!

### *Secondly, not every Christian is expected to have every one of the gifts mentioned*

In both passages Paul speaks very clearly of differing gifts being bestowed upon different people. It is therefore quite wrong for any Christian who possesses one particular gift, or who possesses it in an unusual measure, to insist that his condition is the norm for which others should strive.

### *Thirdly, the gifts of the Spirit are not ours for the asking*

Paul says plainly that while all of the gifts are 'the work of one and the same Spirit', he 'gives them to each man just *as he determines*'. The Holy Spirit is sovereign in the disposal of his gifts, and he deals with us as individuals according to his wisdom and not according to our wishes.

### *Fourthly, no gift is necessarily a mark of spirituality or superiority*

The church at Corinth would appear to have had a

tremendous variety of gifts, including the more remarkable ones, among its membership, but it seems from reading Paul's letter to that particular church that it was perhaps the most spiritually backward in the New Testament. Nowhere in the Bible are we led to believe that ability is a mark of spirituality. The passages we are studying list the *gifts* of the Spirit, not the *rewards* of the Spirit. A man's true spiritual quality is to be judged by his graces, not by his gifts.

### Fifthly, the gifts of the Spirit are never for our own personal enjoyment

Paul tells the Corinthians that these gifts are given 'for the common good'. In the Old Testament, there are several people upon whom the Holy Spirit is said to have come — people like Gideon, Samson, Saul and David — but there is only one who is specifically said to have been 'filled . . . with the Spirit of God' (Exodus 31:3). He was a man by the name of Bezalel, who was endowed with great practical skills. And what was the specific service he was called on to perform? He helped to build the tabernacle in the wilderness! Surely that is more than coincidental, and an excellent illustration! The gifts of the Spirit are never meant for the Christian's own satisfaction, but always for the good of the church, in order that other Christians might be built up in their faith, and helped to become more effective in their lives. In the words of the Apostle Peter, 'Each one should use whatever gift he has received to serve others, faithfully administering God's grace in its various forms' (1 Peter 4:10). Make sure that whatever gift God has given to you is being faithfully used in his service, with the prayer that it might be a continued blessing to other people, and especially to those within the fellowship of the church.

### Constantly thirsty; constantly filled

Scattered throughout the New Testament are specific commandments given to the Christian with regard to the Holy Spirit. We are told 'do not grieve the Holy Spirit of God' (Ephesians 4:30) — and in context the inference is that the Holy Spirit is grieved by any kind of unholy conduct. In another of Paul's letters, we are told 'Do not put out the Spirit's fire' (1 Thessalonians 5:19). The Holy Spirit is like a purifying and illuminating flame in the life of the church, and we are solemnly warned against trying to dampen down his activities. Then we are commanded to 'live by the Spirit' (Galatians 5:16), or, as we might put it, 'keep in step with the Spirit'. This speaks of the need for obedience to everything that the Holy Spirit reveals to us.

But all of these commandments flow out of one crucially important instruction in Paul's letter to the Ephesians, where he says 'Do not get drunk on wine, which leads to debauchery. Instead, *be filled with the Spirit*' (Ephesians 5:18). Here is the ultimate requirement for the Christian in this area, the 'first and great commandment' as far as his relationship with the Holy Spirit is concerned, and we can set out its main meaning by understanding three things about the tense of the verb that is used.

### *In the first place, it is plural*

Just as drunkenness is forbidden for all Christians, so the command to be filled with the Spirit is for all Christians. And as God never commands anything that cannot be attained, this leads us to the exciting truth that every Christian without exception *may* be filled with the Spirit. The fulness of the Spirit is not reserved for New Testament times, or for full-time

ministers, or mature believers. It is available for all
Christians, just as the life-giving sap of the parent tree
is available to fill the tiniest twig as well as the
mightiest branch. The command to be filled with the
Spirit is a thrilling imperative for every believer.

## In the second place, it is passive

We could paraphrase the sentence like this — 'Let the
Holy Spirit fill you'. The fulness of the Spirit is not
something that can be achieved by self-effort, it is
something that comes as we yield ourselves unreservedly to him. The first recorded sin in the New
Testament church was when, as we saw earlier in this
chapter, Ananias and Sapphira kept back some of the
proceeds of the sale of their land. The result for them
was that in the most tragic way possible they missed
all the fulness of blessing that came to the church in
the days that followed. In the same way, the Christian
who keeps back part of his life from the Holy Spirit
will never know the power and the joy of his fulness.

## In the third place, it is present

To grasp the full implications of the sentence, we
would need to amplify it to read 'Keep on letting the
Holy Spirit fill you'. The verb used is in the present
continuous tense. It is not something that any Christian
can claim to have 'done'. He may be able to open his
Bible at Acts 2:21 — which says 'everyone who calls on
the name of the Lord will be saved' — and write a date
in the margin to indicate that that was when he became
a Christian once and for all, but he can never open his
Bible at Ephesians 5:18 and write another date to indicate that that was when he was filled with the Holy
Spirit once and for all. The command is in the present

continuous tense, which means that God wants us to know a present, continuous filling. Here is the real challenge of being a Spirit-filled Christian! It is not trying to reach a spectacular or sensational 'experience' it is the daily discipline of yielding to the control of the Holy Spirit in every area of your life. It is the constant, restless longing to know more and more of God's fulness in your life, and the quiet claiming of Christ's own promise, 'Blessed are those who hunger and thirst for righteousness, for they will be filled' (Matthew 5:6).

## One last word

We began this chapter by saying that the doctrine of the Holy Spirit was one over which there is a great deal of confusion and controversy. That is true, and for that very reason, I want to add this one last word. As you study the subject further, you may find yourself slowly moving towards one or other of the differing schools of thought about the baptism of the Spirit, the gifts of the Spirit, the fulness of the Spirit, and so on. You may find your views hardening into the firm conviction that on this matter or that you have come to the definitive truth, and that other views are wrong. If so, let me beg of you never to substitute what you believe to be accurate theology for what God intends to be a living experience. Never be satisfied with knowing more about the Holy Spirit in your head. Hunger and thirst for more and more of his fulness in your heart and life. Yield every part of your being to his sovereign control, praying constantly that you might be 'filled to the measure of all the fulness of God' (Ephesians 3:19).

## 17. THE WILL OF GOD

It would not be overstating the case to say that in the Christian life nothing is more important than knowing and doing the will of God. It was this fulfilment of the divine purpose that dominated the life of Jesus. He said that he came to earth 'not to do my will but to do the will of him who sent me' (John 6:38), while on another occasion he told his disciples 'My food is to do the will of him who sent me, and to finish his work' (John 4:34). The whole of his earthly life was taken up with the all-consuming aim of fulfilling his heavenly Father's purpose. That fact alone should make the will of God a matter of supreme importance for every Christian.

### Life is not a lottery

In considering the subject of the will of God, it is important first of all to establish that God does *have* a plan for the life of every one of his children – and the Bible makes the point very clear. Paul says that as Christians 'we are God's workmanship, created in Christ Jesus to do good works, which God prepared in advance for us to do' (Ephesians 2:10), while the writer to the Hebrews says that in running the Christian race we are to 'run with perseverance the race marked out for us' (Hebrews 12:1). Life is not a haphazard lottery, uncontrolled and uncontrollable. God has a specific purpose for each one of us, and the fulfilment of that purpose should be the conscious and constant aim of every Christian. Now in the light of all that we have studied so far, we can surely accept that principle without question. To do God's will is not only our overriding but obvious duty. The real issue that is open for discussion is this: *how can I know God's will?* As the Old Testament writer has it, 'A man's steps are directed by the Lord; *how then can any-one understand his own way?'* (Proverbs 20:24). It is that question that we shall seek to answer in this chapter.

## Begin with the obvious

Some people make the mistake of approaching the subject of guidance, or knowing the will of God, in quite the wrong way. When they think of God guiding their lives they immediately think in terms of some kind of unusual revelation. Perhaps as the result of reading some startling incident in the Bible, or a remarkable Christian biography, they begin to expect God to speak to them through dreams or visions, unusual circumstances or spectacular manifestations. Now whilst we can certainly never limit the ways in which God may choose to reveal his will to a Christian, we can state quite positively that God's *normal* methods of guidance are much less spectacular — and just as effective!

For instance, one of God's gifts to the Christian is a developing ability to discern whether a thing is right or wrong. As he grows in grace so his conscience becomes increasingly sensitive, and his judgment increasingly reliable. Now the Bible says that 'The highway of the upright avoids evil' (Proverbs 16:17) — and the Christian's increasing ability to discern good and evil will mean that he will find it increasingly easy to discover where that highway is! This obvious truth about guidance has been badly neglected by many people. Every Christian should praise the Lord for his growing ability to know the essential but sometimes subtle difference between right and wrong — it is one of the greatest means of guidance that he can possibly have. If a thing is right, do it; if it is wrong, avoid it. That is not very spectacular, but it is infallibly effective!

Another obvious factor in guidance is the use of our sanctified common sense. The promise of God's guidance does not mean that we can switch off our minds! While it is true that God tells man that 'As the heavens are higher than the earth, so are my ways higher than your ways and my thoughts than your thoughts' (Isaiah 55:9), that does not mean that man is devoid of common sense, and must always wait for some direct and unusual guidance before he acts. Our daily responsibilities at home, at work, at school or college, all provide us with obvious ways in which we can act safely without any special revelation from God. The businessman whose office opens at 9 a.m. need not spend time gazing into space from 7.30 onwards waiting for God's guidance! The housewife with a sick child, a hungry family or a sinkful of dirty dishes, needs no celestial signwriting to tell her what to do! The wholehearted and honest fulfilment of our social responsibilities is one of the hidden foundations of doing God's will.

## Are you willing?

As we move now into the deeper parts of the subject, we must establish one absolutely crucial factor which affects them all. When some of his listeners expressed astonishment at the quality of his teaching, Jesus told them 'My teaching is not my own. It comes from him who sent me. *If any one chooses to do God's will, he will find out* whether my teaching comes from God or whether I speak on my own'. (John 7:16—17). Notice the words I have deliberately emphasised! Here is a bedrock principle, not only in the particular context in which Jesus spoke, but in the wider and general area of guidance. Jesus made it crystal clear that before a person could be given theological discernment, he would need to have spiritual desire. Before a man could understand whether the words of Jesus were truly the words of God, he would need to be willing to obey them.

God never wastes truth on a man unwilling to receive it — and he never gives guidance to a man who is not prepared to follow it. The greatest responsibility a man has in the issue of guidance is to be willing to obey God's will, whatever it may be, wherever it may lead, and whatever it may cost. God has not promised to disclose his will to any except those who are willing to do it. Every Christian needs constantly to face up to this tremendous challenge.

### Meekness is a must

I am often asked questions about guidance, and on almost every occasion, I turn the enquirer to Psalm 25, because it contains some of the clearest principles on guidance in the whole Bible. In verse 9, for instance, we have these absolutely pivotal words — 'He guides the humble in what is right and teaches them his way'. We began this chapter by saying that nothing was more important than knowing and doing the will of God. Now here is a verse that says that God *does* guide certain people, that he *does* teach them his way. Here, surely, is the promise for which we have been looking — guidance guaranteed! But notice that there is a condition. The people God promises to guide are defined as *'the humble'*, and it is therefore vitally important that we understand what this means.

The clearest explanation of the word translated here as 'humble' comes in another of the Psalms which includes the subject of guidance. In it, God says 'I will instruct you and teach you in the way you should go; I will counsel you and watch over you. Do not be like the horse or the mule, which have no understanding but must be controlled by bit and bridle or they will not come to you' (Psalm 32:8—9). In these two verses God says that in order to know his guidance we are to avoid being like either a horse or a mule. Now the characteristics of a horse are that it is proud, head-strong, adventurous and independent. If you have ever tried to break in a horse you will know that it can be a dangerous business! The characteristics of a mule, on the other hand, are exactly the opposite — it is stub-born, dour, resistant. The horse has to be restrained from running wild; the mule has to be pushed and prodded before it will move at all; *and the Christian is to be like neither!* In order to claim the promise of God's guidance the Christian must neither dash ahead of God in self-centred enthusiasm, nor lag behind in hesitant unbelief. He must be willing not only to go in God's direction, but to do so at God's speed and in God's time.

## The importance of being obedient

Another bedrock principle in the question of guidance comes in two of the best-known verses in the Old Testament — 'Trust in the Lord with all your heart, and lean not on your own understanding; *in all your ways acknowledge him,* and he will make your paths straight' (Proverbs 3:5—6). Here again we have a clear promise of guidance, but once more it is conditional, and this time the condition is 'in all your ways acknowledge him'. In other words, God promises to give further guidance to those who are obeying guidance already received. Imagine that you had to make a 100 mile car journey by night. Before starting to move, you would switch on the headlights, which would illuminate, say, 60 feet of the road in front of you. All of the rest of the 100 miles would be in total darkness as far as you were concerned; in fact, everything more than 60 feet away would be hidden from your sight. Only as you began to move along the road would the area beyond that initial 60 feet come into vision. So in the question of guidance it is only as we go along the road which God illuminates for us that we will receive light on the next part of the journey. To illustrate from the Bible, it was only when Paul obeyed the Lord's command to 'go into the city' (Acts 9:6) at the time of his conversion on the Damascus road that he was shown the next part of the journey that eventually took him throughout Palestine, Syria, Asia Minor, Greece, Cyprus and Italy in the service of the gospel. It has been said that a literal rendering of the Hebrew version of Proverbs 4:12 would be 'As you go step by step I will open up the way before you'. Only as we are obedient to that part of God's will that he has revealed to us will we be given any further relevation. God only promises to give more light to those who walk in the light they have! Are you frustrated at not knowing God's will in some area of your life? If so, could it be because you are being disobedient over some issue that he has already made clear? If that is the case, the answer to your frustration lies in your own hands!

## The infallible guide

We can now turn to look at some of the normal ways in which God guides the Christian, and the first and foremost of these is unquestionably his own word, the Bible. Keeping to the same picture of illumination, the Psalmist says 'Your word is a lamp to my feet and a light for my path' (Psalm 119:105). A few verses later he adds 'Direct my footsteps according to your word;

let no sin rule over me' (Psalm 119:133). The Bible is God's infallible and unchanging word, and as such it can be trusted at all times and in all situations. Now this does not mean that it is like an encyclopaedia of good living, containing detailed guidance on every situation that is ever likely to crop up in your life; but it does contain all the essential principles to guide and govern your living. It is not like an ordnance survey, with every minute geographical detail shown in its correct position; but it is a perfectly accurate map of the whole area to be covered, with the main through routes clearly marked out. Within the pages of the Bible you will discover all that you need to know on this earth about God, man, sin, salvation, holiness, death, and the life beyond. God's word contains everything that a person needs to know to guide him into a holy, happy and helpful Christian life, as we shall see in more detail in the next chapter.

But if this is true, how should we use the Bible in the matter of guidance? Certainly not as a 'lucky dip', opening the Bible at random and hoping that a verse will stand out of the page and answer all our problems. I have a friend who says that his Bible naturally falls open at Judges 3 in the Old Testament and 2 Thessalonians 2 in the New Testament — but he knows that this is not guidance but a faulty binding! Now God does sometimes take a verse or passage 'out of the blue' and impress it upon a person's heart so vividly that they have no doubt that they are being divinely guided, but we need to remember that *this is not his normal method.* We should seek to conduct our lives along the principles of 'the whole will of God' (Acts 20:27) and not by bits and pieces picked out at moments of sudden need. That leads on to a second important thing about our use of the Bible, which is that we should not wait for a crisis to come before learning the principles it contains. Even before the days of radar, the captains of vessels using the notorious Inner Passage off the coast of British Columbia and Alaska negotiated the hundreds of miles of tortuous seaway with scarcely an accident. They steered their ships through the changing tides and dense fogs by sounding their ships' sirens and judging the distance from the nearest cliff-face by the time the echo took to reach them. But they could only do this in the fog because they had already done it time without number in clear weather, and made a careful record of all the relevant data. The Christian best able to steer his way safely through dark and difficult times is the one who has made a constant habit of studying the Bible and storing its truth in his mind and heart.

### Ask God!

The Apostle James gives us the next positive way in which we can know the guidance of God when he says 'If any of you lacks wisdom, he should ask God, who gives generously to all without finding fault, and it will be given to him' (James 1:5). The Amplified Bible translates part of that sentence 'let him ask of *the giving* God', and this helps to point us to the great truth that God not only has a plan for our lives, but that he is willing to reveal it to us. We are not to think of prayer for guidance as trying to squeeze information out of a reluctant stranger, but rather as a simple, confident request made to a loving Father. Jesus made this so clear in the Sermon on the Mount, when he told his disciples, 'Ask and it will be given to you; seek and you will find; knock and the door will be opened to you. For everyone who asks receives; he who seeks finds; and to him who knocks, the door will be opened. Which of you, if his son asks for bread, will give him a stone? Or if he asks for a fish, will give him a snake? If you, then, though you are evil, know how to give good gifts to your children, *how much more* will your Father in heaven give good gifts to those who ask him!' (Matthew 7:7—11). Mark that carefully! The picture is clear and the answers to the questions obvious! And surely those 'good things' include clear guidance when it is needed? Uncomplicated faith in God's willingness to guide us is a vital factor in a healthy attitude towards the subject of divine guidance.

### The gentle whisper

When Jesus promised that the Holy Spirit would come to his disciples, he specifically told them that 'when he, the Spirit of truth, comes, he will guide you into all truth' (John 16:13). In the immediate context, this promise had to do with doctrine, but as we see later in the New Testament, it also included the practical direction of their lives. At one point, we are told that Paul and his companions were 'kept by the Holy Spirit from preaching the word in the province of Asia' (Acts 16:6). Luke then goes on to say that 'When they came to the border of Mysia, they tried to enter Bithynia, but the Spirit of Jesus would not allow them to' (Acts 16:7). We could actually paraphrase this 'They tried again and again to go into Bithynia, but the Holy Spirit put his foot down and refused!' We are not told why this should be so, but Paul and his friends were obviously convinced that the Holy Spirit was speaking to them. There was 'a gentle whisper' (1 Kings 19:12), and they knew that it was the voice of God, putting a stop to their plans, changing their itinerary. Then, following (in this case) a remarkable vision by Paul, Luke says that 'we got ready at once to leave for Macedonia, concluding that God had called us to preach the gospel to them. From Troas we put out to sea and sailed straight for Samothrace, and the next day on to Neapolis' (Acts 16:10—11). They came to a place free from obstacles by means of obstacles! Only because of the pressure of divine limitations did they come to a place of divine liberty! The vision and the voice turned confusion into conviction, and frustration into fruitfulness! The Bible says that Christians should habitually be 'led by the Spirit of God' (Romans 8:14) which means that we should constantly be learning to listen for his voice. But let me add a word of caution here. Beware of treating *all* 'feelings' as if they are the voice of the Holy Spirit. In another context, but equally true here, John says 'do not believe every spirit, but test the spirits to see whether they are from God' (1 John 4:1). One sure way of doing this is to remember that the Holy Spirit never guides contrary to the teaching of the Holy Scriptures. To give one simple example, the Holy Spirit will never guide a Christian to marry a non-Christian, because the Bible says 'Do not be yoked together with unbelievers' (2 Corinthians 6:14). If a Christian says he 'feels led' to do such a thing, then we can be sure that his leading is diabolical and not divine. Learn to test the word behind your ear by the word in front of your eyes!

## Wait for it

There is so much more that could be said about the subject of guidance, but space will not allow us to develop it any further. There is, however, one final thing we should add, and that is that guidance is not always instant; as we have just seen, it was certainly not so in the case of Paul and his friends in Asia Minor.

For his own wise purposes, God sometimes delays revealing his will, even on an important issue, but because 'his way is perfect' (Psalm 18:30), we should always be grateful when he does! Just as a glass of cloudy water becomes clear when we wait for the sediment to settle, so many of our troublesome situations will only become clarified as we allow God time to work and to speak. There are times in our lives when urgent, immediate action is needed — and God will never fail us in the hour of crisis; but there are more situations than we think when we need to remember God's promise that 'In repentance and rest is your salvation, in quietness and trust is your strength' (Isaiah 30:15).

# Eight — Enjoying my fellowship

### 18. THE BIBLE

At the very beginning of these studies we took the position that the Bible is precisely what it claims to be — 'the living and enduring word of God' (1 Peter 1:23) — and every page since then has been written with the conviction that the Bible is man's final written authority in all matters of belief and behaviour. In this chapter, we are not going to try to prove this, although volumes could be written to show the truthfulness of the Bible's claim. For the determined unbeliever, no amount of proof is sufficient, and for the believer who has a living experience of the Bible's truth, no further proof is necessary! Instead, we shall concentrate on the place of the Bible in the daily life of the Christian.

## The word of life

Paul calls the Bible 'the word of life' (Philippians 2:16), and we have already seen something of the truth of this as we have gone through these studies together.

### It leads men to new life

The Christian life begins with the new birth, and Peter says (to complete the quotation above), that we were 'born again, not of perishable seed, but of imperishable, through the living and enduring word of God' (1 Peter 1:23). James says exactly the same kind of thing — '(God) chose to give us birth through the word of truth, that we might be a kind of first-fruits of all he created' (James 1:18). Men come to know God in many different situations and circumstances, but always through the communication of the message contained in the Bible, what Paul calls 'the word of truth, the gospel of your salvation' (Ephesians 1:13).

### It leads men to clean life

We saw this very clearly in the chapter on sanctification. Only as a person regulates his life according to the teaching of the Bible can he live in a way that is pleasing to God. The Psalmist was able to say 'I have hidden your word in my heart that I might not sin against you' (Psalm 119:11).

### It leads men to strong life

In one of the greatest statements ever made about God's word, David says 'The law of the Lord is perfect, reviving the soul. The statutes of the Lord are trustworthy, making wise the simple. The precepts of the Lord are right, giving joy to the heart. The commands of the Lord are radiant, giving light to the eyes. The fear of the Lord is pure, enduring for ever. The ordinances of the Lord are sure and altogether righteous' (Psalm 19:7–9). The person whose life is ribbed with the principles of God's word is going to stand out as a tower of strength in a world of moral and spiritual weaklings!

### It leads men to confident life

The Apostle Paul says that 'everything that was written in the past was written to teach us, so that through endurance and the encouragement of the Scriptures we might have hope' (Romans 15:4). The Bible not only gives a man the clearest view of history and the most balanced assessment of contemporary life, it also gives him settled assurance about his eternal destiny, enabling him to live a life of joyful confidence.

In all of these areas, then, the Bible proves itself to be 'the word of life'. But how can we sum up its place in the daily life of the Christian? Perhaps the simplest way of all is to take the very common analogy of eating.

## Food for the soul

It is interesting to notice how often in the Bible the word of God is likened to food. The Psalmist says 'How sweet are your promises to my taste, sweeter than honey to my mouth!' (Psalm 119:103). The prophet Jeremiah says 'When your words came, I ate them; they were my joy and my heart's delight' (Jeremiah 15:16). God directed Ezekiel to prophesy with the words 'Son of man, eat what is before you, eat this scroll; then go and speak to the house of Israel' (Ezekiel 3:1). In resisting the devil in the wilderness, Jesus said 'Man does not live on bread alone, but on every word that comes from the mouth of God' (Matthew 4:4). Peter tells those young in the faith that 'Like newborn babes' they are to 'crave pure spiritual milk, so that by it you may grow up in your salvation, now that you have tasted that the Lord is good' (1 Peter 2:2—3). The writer to the Hebrews, disappointed that they had made such little progress in spiritual things, tells them that 'though by this time you ought to be teachers, you need someone to teach you the elementary truths of God's word all over again. You need milk, not solid food' (Hebrews 5:12). What food is to the physical life, the Bible is to the spiritual life, and from that straightforward analogy we can draw a number of simple but important lessons.

**Regular meals**

It goes without saying that the person who neglects his food ultimately endangers his physical health, and by the same token the person who neglects feeding on the Word of God is bound to suffer spiritually. In the physical world, the main results of diet deficiency are lack of appetite, stunted growth, deformed features, and susceptibility to disease, and every single one of those could be applied in a spiritual sense to the Christian who neglects his Bible. Lack of appetite? — In a strange and tragic way lack of Bible intake leads to lack of Bible desire. What a contrast to that remarkable man Job, who was able to say 'My feet have closely followed (God's) steps; I have kept to his way without turning aside. I have not departed from the commands of his lips; I have treasured the words of his mouth more than my daily bread' (Job 23:11—12). Stunted growth? — When Paul left the church at Ephesus he told the elders there 'I commit you to God and to the word of his grace, which can build you up' (Acts 20:32). Show me the Christian who has no spiritual muscle, and I will show you the Christian who is neglecting God's word. Deformed features? — Good food makes a vital contribution to good health, which shows in the shape of the body, the texture of the skin; and if a man is going to lead a balanced and attractive life he will need to feed his soul wisely. Susceptibility to disease? — The Sadducees got themselves into all kinds of trouble because, as Jesus told them 'you do not know the Scriptures' (Mark 12:24). Has any of this challenged you? Are you feeding regularly on the word of God? Is your intake sufficient to keep you spiritually healthy? If you are going without at least one meal a day you are living dangerously! Having said that, we must by no means get into bondage about precisely when we should read our Bibles, or how long we should spend in Bible study every day, any more than we need to be legalistic about sitting down to eat at exactly the same times every day, or taking the same number of minutes over each meal. These are matters which every person must decide for himself. He will certainly need to take his daily schedule into consideration, and he may also need to consider his age, his maturity, his ability to study, and the particular needs of his Christian service. The all-important thing is not that your spiritual meals are regimented, but that they are regular, and sufficient to keep you well nourished.

## A balanced diet

In recent years, a great deal has been discovered about the specific and comparative values of vitamins, protein, carbohydrates, minerals and other constituents of ordinary food. We now know that each of these plays a particular part in sustaining and strengthening body tissues, blood, bone, muscle and so on. We also know that an unbalanced diet can cause as much damage as an insufficient one. Boiled potatoes may be fine, but boiled potatoes alone three times a day would soon have their effect! In spiritual eating, the same principles hold good. The Bible is not only unequalled in *value* as spiritual food, it is also unequalled in its perfectly balanced *variety*. It contains history, biography, poetry, prophecy, philosophy and theology. Parts of it were written by famous people, and parts by people who were almost unknown. They came from different countries, lived at different times, spoke different languages, and expressed themselves in different ways, although always with divine authority. The result is a storehouse of different but related truth, a larder full of fascinating food. Make sure that you make the most of it! Beware of reading only the New Testament and ignoring the Old, or vice-versa. Never stay too long in any one part of the Bible. And never make the mistake of reading only those parts of the Bible which appeal to you — remember that '*All scripture* is God-breathed and is useful for teaching, rebuking, correcting and training in righteousness, so that the man of God may be thoroughly equipped for every good work' (2 Timothy 3:16). A friend of mine was once the thinnest boy in his class at school, but later became the holder of a number of national weightlifting records. He told me that one of the secrets of his success was that he began to eat wisely and well, carefully ensuring that his diet included all those things calculated to strengthen his body. The lesson for the Christian is obvious!

Work out a system of your own, or follow some published guide to Bible reading, that will ensure that you are not missing any of the truth that God has provided for your spiritual nourishment.

## The importance of digestion

In the physical world we have become increasingly aware of the value of good digestion, and of the many disorders that can gradually develop because of bad eating habits. The spiritual parallel is the danger of hurriedly glancing at a Bible passage and then dashing off to do something else. Sooner or later, that kind of thing leads to trouble! To benefit fully from food, we need to eat it, masticate it and digest it, and we will only get the benefit we need from the word of God by reading, study and meditation. We need to read the Bible straightforwardly to get the facts, study it seriously to get the meaning, and meditate upon it slowly to get the benefit! If your daily reading consists of quite a small passage, then read it over at least twice, more times if necessary. If you find it genuinely helpful, read it in more than one carefully selected version. Of the many that are available today the *New International Version* may well be the very finest with high standards of reliability and readability, two reasons why I have made exclusive use of it in this book. For daily reading, use one of the published systems as a general guide; for study, get hold of a reliable commentary to help you to dig out the technical facts, precise meanings of words, and so on; and for meditation, rely on neither! Learn instead to trust God's promise that the Holy Spirit who indwells you will 'guide you into all truth' (John 16:13). With the Psalmist, learn to come directly to God with the prayer 'Open my eyes that I may see wonderful things in your law' (Psalm 119:18). As you meditate on the passage you have read, try to discover whether there is a new truth for you to learn, a promise for you to claim, a commandment for you to obey, a warning for you to heed, a challenge for you to face, action for you to take. Allow the word of God to get into your spiritual bloodstream so that it will find expression in your practical behaviour!

## Beyond the page to the person

Here, the analogy breaks down, as even the best of illustrations tend to do when applied to spiritual truth. When we eat our meals there is no need to establish any kind of relationship with the people who grew, harvested, packed, prepared or delivered the food. But in coming to the Bible, establishing and developing a relationship with its heavenly Author is essential. One of the most important things you can ever learn about the Bible is that for all of its accuracy, its truth, its magnificence, and its glory, *it is not an end in itself.* There is a perfect illustration of this in John 5, when Jesus was answering critics who refused to believe his claim to be divine. After giving several proofs that his claim was true, he went on 'You diligently study the Scriptures because you think that by them you possess eternal life. These are the Scriptures that testify about me, yet you refuse to come to me to have life' (John 5:39—40). Read that through very carefully! These people were diligent Bible readers, and their reason for reading the Old Testament scriptures was so that they might receive eternal life. But what they failed to do was to put their trust in the One of whom the scriptures spoke, with the result that their efforts were in vain. As you come to the Bible, determine above everything else that you are going to get beyond the page to the person. Never be satisfied with merely gaining knowledge, storing information, analysing truth, or remembering facts. The word of God is meant to lead you to the God of the word. Hosea's cry was not merely 'Let us acknowledge the Lord' but *'let us press on to acknowledge him'* (Hosea 6:3) — the perfect attitude for today's Christian!

## 19. PRAYER

One of the most significant requests his disciples ever made to Jesus was when they asked him 'Lord, teach us to pray' (Luke 11:1). Today, nearly 2,000 years later, every honest Christian would admit to the same need. Although we all believe that prayer is not only right and good but important and essential, very few of us would admit to being much beyond the kindergarten stage in our understanding or experience. Yet the Bible is crammed with exhortations, instructions, examples, promises and warnings on the subject, and we must turn to its teaching again and again. In this chapter I want us to concentrate not so much on the 'mechanics' of prayer, but on the principles that govern it, although of course the one eventually flows into the other.

## Two way communication

To put it in the simplest way possible, we could say that the Bible is the word of God to man. It is one of the primary ways in which God the Creator speaks to his creatures. In the same way, we could define prayer as the word of man to God, but, in this case we could add that it is the *only* way in which the creature can speak to his Creator. There is no other way in which a man can communicate with God, or initiate any deepening of his fellowship with him. To understand that is immediately to raise prayer far above the level of a kind of spiritual shopping-list, which is how many people think of it. Prayer is much more than that. It is a divinely-given means of developing a relationship, not a man-made scheme for delivering requests. And that immediately raises a challenge that can be put in the form of a simple but searching question: *how much would you pray if there were not things you needed*? If your honest answer is 'Very little', then it probably betrays a defective understanding of what prayer is meant to be, and what it is meant to achieve. This chapter is written to help in meeting that need.

## The lines are open now

One of the most important things to grasp about prayer is also one of the simplest, namely, that prayer is *possible.* That may sound too obvious for words, but I believe that it not only needs to be said, it needs to be emphasised and explained. From my own experience, and from talking with other Christians, I am convinced that one of the greatest hindrances to prayer comes when a person feels that they are not 'ready' to pray. They feel unprepared, or out of touch, or spiritually below par, with the result that they decide to give prayer a miss until they feel in a better frame of mind. I have put that as simply as I possibly can, but I am sure that for many Christians it will ring deeply true. Yet to act in that way is to fall for one of 'the devil's schemes' (Ephesians 6:11), and to ignore one of the Bible's greatest truths. At the very moment when Jesus died on the cross, we read that back in Jerusalem, 'the curtain of the temple was torn in two from top to bottom' (Matthew 27:51). This beautiful curtain made of 'blue, purple and scarlet yarn and finely-twisted linen, with cherubim worked into it' (Exodus 26:31), hung between the Holy Place and the Holy of Holies, the inner sanctuary of the temple. Only the High Priest could pass beyond the curtain, and then only once a year, and under very special conditions, including a ritualistic animal sacrifice. The curtain symbolised the fact that because of his sin man was barred from coming into God's holy presence. But when Jesus died on the cross, and in doing so 'offered for all time one sacrifice for sins' (Hebrews 10:12), the curtain was miraculously torn apart by an act of God. *The symbolic barrier was ripped as a sign that the sin barrier had been removed.* Sharing this great truth some time later, the writer to the Hebrews said 'Therefore, brothers, since *we have confidence to enter the Most Holy Place* by the blood of Jesus, by new and living way opened for us through the curtain, that is, his body, and since we have a great priest over the house of God, *let us draw near to God with a sincere heart in full assurance of faith'* (Hebrews 10:19—22).

Notice the words I have deliberately emphasised! The Bible says that the Christian can approach God with confidence, with a full assurance of faith, because Christ has died to put away the one thing that had previously prevented him, his sin: *and he can do so at any time.* Any Christian who understands that he is justified by faith alone already knows that he does not need an ecclesiastical ceremony, a religious ritual, the offering of a sacrifice, or the mediation of any other person, dead or alive, in order to pray — but neither does he need to bring himself up to a particular spiritual pitch. To think that he does is to miss the whole point of the torn curtain, and of the tremendous truths explained in Hebrews 10. If Christians could only pray when they were worthy to do so, God would still be waiting for the first call! The exhilarating fact is that the way is now open for every Christian to pray at any time, in any place, and in any frame of mind. In recent years, there has been a rapid development of 'phone-in' programmes on radio and television. In this way, listeners and viewers have been able to share 'live' in discussion monitored in a central studio. Shortly before a 'phone-in' programme, an announcement is usually made that the telephone lines will be open to receive calls during a certain limited time, and only calls received during that period can be accepted. For the Christian, needing to get through to God, *the lines are open now!* Whatever your situation, however you feel, whatever your problem, let nothing keep you back from prayer, and from knowing that because of the death of Jesus on your behalf, you can have instant and constant access to your Father in heaven.

## Praise the Lord!

In trying now to summarise the things that should form the content of a Christian's prayer life, we must begin not with an application for gifts but with the adoration of the Giver! In the words of the Psalmist 'Great is the Lord, and most worthy of praise; his greatness no one can fathom' (Psalm 145:3). That being so, no Christian need ever run out of things to say when he prays! The more you read your Bible, the more you will learn of the majesty, the glory, the holiness, the greatness, the wisdom, the mercy and the love of God; and the more you learn of these, the more you will find yourself wanting to obey David's invitation, 'Glorify the Lord with me; let us exalt his name together' (Psalm 34:3). And to hear God say 'He who sacrifices thank offerings honours me' (Psalm 50:23) only gives you an added incentive! But praise and worship soon lead on to thanksgiving, and it is striking to notice how often, in the New Testament alone, we are encouraged to praise and thank God for his goodness, his love, his mercy, and his provision of all our needs. Paul says that we should be 'always giving thanks to God the Father for everything in the name of our Lord Jesus Christ' (Ephesians 5:20). He says we are to 'Devote yourselves to prayer, being watchful and thankful' (Colossians 4:2) and that as Christians we should be 'overflowing with thankfulness' (Colossians 2:7). As a frequent visitor to other people's homes, few things grieve me more than children's ingratitude to parents, and few things please me more than happy thankfulness for kindness shown. The same is true in the Christian family, for having told us to 'Be joyful always; pray continually' and 'give thanks in all circumstances', Paul goes on to say 'for this is God's will for you in Christ Jesus' (1 Thessalonians 5:16—18).

Ingratitude is disobedience! Just as the beauty of God can never exhaust our praise, so the blessings of God can never exhaust our thanksgiving! I know of few things more heartening, encouraging or strengthening, than to spend the last conscious moments of a day going through the scores of things for which I have had cause to be grateful since I got up that morning. Health and strength, food and clothing, home and shelter, family and friends, safety in travelling, acts of kindness, an unexpected gift, help given in my work; the list is endless. The events of even one hour in the day would take almost as long to remember in detail — and for all of them I can praise the Lord. Above all, and every day, I can meditate on the wonder of my salvation in Christ and say with the Apostle Paul, 'Thanks be to God for his indescribable gift!' (2 Corinthians 9:15).

### Confession is good for the soul

No Christian can spend long praising God for his majesty and glory, and thanking him for his goodness, before sensing something of his own moral and spiritual shortcomings. The Apostle John says bluntly 'If we claim to be without sin, we deceive ourselves, and the truth is not in us' (1 John 1:8), and while that is a verse that we often (and rightly) use when speaking to unbelievers, it is important to notice that it was originally written to Christians. But immediately after that sober statement of fact comes this wonderful promise — 'If we confess our sins, (God) is faithful and just and will forgive us our sins, and purify us from all unrighteousness' (1 John 1:9). The word 'confess' means 'to name together', and to confess our sins means bringing them out into the open and agreeing with what God says about them. Confession can therefore be costly, and is always humbling — but only as we are prepared to acknowledge our sins of word, thought and deed can we know God's complete and free forgiveness. Learn to admit the facts, and to claim the promise!

## The perfect prayer

When the disciples asked to be taught how to pray, Jesus replied with the words of what we call 'The Lord's Prayer'. Over the centuries these words have become the most familiar in the whole Bible, and they are a perfect summary of the 'asking' part of prayer. The six petitions of the prayer cover three areas and in general ask for three specific things. Following the slightly fuller wording in Matthew's Gospel, notice carefully what they are.

### Firstly, that God's glory might be seen

'Our Father in heaven, hallowed be your name, your kingdom come, your will be done on earth as it is in heaven' (Matthew 6:9—10). Those words already cover three out of the six petitions, yet there is no mention of even one specific need of the person who is praying! The great over-riding concern of these three petitions is God's glory; they are concerned with the honouring of his name, the coming of his kingdom, the doing of his will. If we were to examine them in detail, and study other passages in the Bible that touch on the same subjects, we would certainly see that these prayers embrace international affairs, the welfare of our own nation, the state of the church, revival, evangelism, and our own personal reaction to adverse circumstances, to name but a few, but the important thing is to notice what is their main concern, namely, that God's glory might be seen. Later on in the same chapter Jesus said 'Seek first (God's) kingdom and his righteousness' (Matthew 6:33). How does your prayer life stand up to that principle? Does God come first? — his glory, his cause, his interests? It is dangerously possible to pray for the right things in the wrong way, and for the wrong reasons. The Apostle James says 'When you ask, you do not receive, because you ask with wrong motives, that you may spend what you get on your pleasures' (James 4:3). In all of your prayers make sure that your motives are right, and that your over-riding concern is that God's glory might be seen.

### Secondly, that God's goodness might be shown

'Give us today our daily bread' (Matthew 6:11). This simple prayer acknowledges that we are dependent upon God for everything in life, even the food we eat day by day. As Paul told the people of Athens '(God) himself gives all men life and breath and everything else' (Acts 17:25). In an age when man is professing to be increasingly self-sufficient nothing is healthier for the Christian than a daily recognition that he is utterly dependent upon God, not only for his spiritual needs, but for his physical, mental and material requirements.

### Thirdly, that God's grace might be sent

'Forgive us our debts, as we also have forgiven our debtors. And lead us not into temptation, but deliver us from the evil one' (Matthew 6:12—13). These two petitions both deal with the same subject — sin. They speak of the forgiveness of our own sins, our forgiveness of the sins of others, our being kept from the temptation to sin, and our being kept free from harm at the hands of the devil, who is the author of sin. This concentration of thought immediately tells us a central truth about the Christian life, and that is that nothing is more important than our moral character. Whether we are rich or poor, healthy or sick, famous or unknown, talented or 'ordinary' — these things are irrelevant. What matters above all else is that we are kept free from sin and made 'holy and blameless in (God's) sight' (Ephesians 1:4) — and only the grace of God can achieve that for us!

One final point on The Lord's Prayer: notice that all the petitions are in the plural. No man can pray properly who prays selfishly. There are multitudes of people in the world who need your prayers, and scores of them are within your daily orbit at home, at work, in your social life, at church, at school, and so on. If necessary, devise a written system for ensuring that those for whom God gives you a special concern are prayed for regularly, and for them as well as for yourself, 'Look to the Lord and his strength; seek his face always' (1 Chronicles 16:11).

### Never give up

Immediately after teaching his disciples The Lord's Prayer, Jesus went on to tell the story of a man who knocked on a friend's door at midnight and asked if he could borrow three loaves of bread. His friend was already in bed and reluctant to get up, but the man at the door refused to leave until he got what he came for. Applying the moral of the story to the subject of prayer, Jesus went on to say 'So I say to you: Ask and it will be given to you; seek and you will find; knock and the door will be opened to you' (Luke 11:9). The force of the verbs Jesus used means that we could translate them 'Ask and keep on asking; seek and keep on seeking; knock and keep on knocking' — bringing out the point Jesus was making about persistence in prayer. It is so easy to pray for a thing once or twice, and then to give up when nothing happens. It is so easy to pray for a friend's conversion for a month or two, and then to lose heart when they seem to show no interest in spiritual things. But the promise Jesus is making here is not that every prayer will be answered immediately and in the way we want, but rather that there are many issues about which we will need to pray faithfully and for a long time before God appears to answer. The lesson we need to learn is that delay is not denial. God's timing is as perfect as his working, and we must learn to trust him even when we cannot understand why he allows certain situations to develop without apparently taking any action. When Lazarus, a personal friend of Jesus, fell ill, his sisters Mary and Martha immediately sent word to him, but he deliberately delayed coming to Bethany until four days after Lazarus had died. To everyone, that must have seemed a complete refusal of the two sisters' request, but as we read the story through, culminating in the tremendous moment when Jesus raised Lazarus from the dead, we discover that he delayed his coming for two reasons – 'for God's glory so that God's Son may be glorified through it' (John 11:4), and 'so that you may believe' (John 11:15). Looking back on the story, it is easy now to see that raising Lazarus from the dead made a much greater impact than healing his sickness would have done – but it is not always easy in our own lives to remain faithful in prayer when the answer seems no nearer. Yet the Bible says that we 'should always pray and not give up' (Luke 18:1). God only delays his answers when it is best to do so, when the delayed answer is for his glory and for our good. No Christian should complain at that!

### 'Mayday!'

In the world of communication, 'Mayday!' (from the French 'M'aider!', meaning 'Help me!') is recognised as the international distress call, one immediately answered by a ship or aircraft of any nationality. So far in this chapter, we have been thinking about prayer in the general, daily sense, but there are also situations in the Christian life that call not for disciplined prayer over months and years, but a sudden cry of 'Mayday!' We have two perfect examples of this in Matthew's Gospel. On the first occasion, Jesus was asleep on board the disciples' boat on the Sea of Galilee when a sudden storm arose and threatened to drown them all. The terrified disciples woke him and cried 'Lord save us! We're going to drown!' (Matthew 8:25). On the second occasion Jesus invited Peter to walk towards him on the surface of the sea. Peter responded immediately, but 'when he saw the wind, he was afraid and, beginning to sink, cried out "Lord, save me"' (Matthew 14:30). In both cases the need was serious and obvious, the 'prayer' was simple and urgent – and the answer was immediate and complete.

One great lesson to learn from these incidents is that nothing ever takes God unawares. With him, there are no unforeseen circumstances, no 'panic stations'; and because he understands our frailty so well, we can know that he is always tuned in on the 'Mayday!' waveband, ready to hear and answer our emergency calls. What an encouragement it is to know that nothing is out of ultimate control, because nothing is out of his control! No wonder the writer to the Hebrews says 'Let us then approach the throne of grace with confidence, so that we may receive mercy and find grace to help us in our time of need' (Hebrews 4:16).

## The prayer that never fails

The Christian is not only free to pray at any time and in any place, but also on any subject. There is no area of life which cannot be taken to God in prayer, asking for his help, his blessing, his guidance, or his enabling. There is no issue so big that God cannot cope with it — 'Is anything too hard for the Lord?' (Genesis 18:14); and no issue so small that God does not care about it — 'the very hairs of your head are all numbered' (Matthew 10:30). But does God always answer the Christian's prayer in the affirmative, even if the answer is sometimes delayed? Obviously not — but as we read the New Testament, we discover that there is one particular kind of prayer that is always successful. Jesus mentioned it several times in the course of his talk to the disciples following their last meal together before his crucifixion, and because it is obviously such an important matter, we would do well to read exactly what he said before going any further. Firstly, he said 'I will do whatever you ask *in my name,* so that the Son may bring glory to the Father. You may ask me for anything *in my name,* and I will do it' (John 14:13—14). Later, he told them that 'the Father will give you whatever you ask *in my name'* (John 15:16) and underlined this some time afterwards by adding 'I tell you the truth, my Father will give you whatever you ask *in my name'* (John 16:23). From those statements it is clear that the all-important thing in prayer is not that we pray at great length, nor even that we pray often; nor is it that we use certain phraseology or adopt any particular physical position. The one critical factor in prayer is that we pray in the name of the Lord Jesus. Now to pray in the name of Jesus does not merely mean adding 'we ask it in the name of Jesus' to the end of our prayers. It means praying according to his nature; in other words praying as he would pray in the same situation. But that means praying according to God's will, and it is precisely for that reason that prayer offered in the name of Jesus can never fail to reach its objective. As John says so clearly, 'This is the assurance we have in approaching God; that if we ask anything *according to his will* he hears us. And if we know that he hears us — whatever we ask — we know that we have what we asked of him' (1 John 5:14—15).

But can any man — even a mature Christian — do that? Left to himself, no; but the Bible has the answer to that problem, too, for while even Paul admits that 'we do not know what we ought to pray' he immediately adds 'but the Spirit himself intercedes for us with groans that words cannot express. And he who searches our hearts knows the mind of the Spirit, because the Spirit intercedes for the saints in accordance with God's will' (Romans 8:26—27). Only as the Holy Spirit prompts us will we pray according to God's will, and experience the truth of the Bible's promise that 'The prayer of a righteous man is powerful and effective' (James 5:16).

This means that we are as dependent upon God for our prayers as we are for his answers! But it also means that while it is obviously true that prayer affects the rest of your life, it is equally true that the rest of life affects your prayer. It is only as you 'Delight yourself in the Lord' that he will 'give you the desires of your heart (Psalm 37:4). Only as a Christian is living in close fellowship with God will he recognise the Spirit's voice and be able to pray more and more in line with God's 'good, pleasing and perfect will' (Romans 12:2). Happy the Christian who is doing that! For him, the promise of Jesus is a living reality — 'Until now you have not asked for anything in my name. Ask and you will receive and your joy will be complete' (John 16:24).

## 20. THE CHURCH

When a child is born into the world it automatically becomes a member of a human family. It has no choice in the matter, nor can it choose its brothers or sisters; its membership of that family is the immediate and natural result of its birth. In the spiritual world, exactly the same principles apply. As we saw in an earlier chapter, the only way in which a person can become a Christian is to be 'born again' (John 3:3) — and at the very moment of that re-birth he enters God's spiritual family and becomes a member of what Paul calls 'God's household' (Ephesians 2:19). It is on this family or household — best-known as 'the church' — that we are going to focus our attention in this final chapter.

### The word that says it all

When people speak about 'the church' today, they usually have one of three things in mind. The word is sometimes used as a very loose description of world-wide religion. At other times, people use it to describe the clergy or the ecclesiastical hierarchy — they speak of trainee clergymen as 'going into the church'. Thirdly, and most often, the word is used to define certain buildings in which people meet to worship. Now it is interesting to notice that although the word occurs over 100 times in the New Testament, and its equivalent over 70 times in the Old Testament, it is never used in any one of those three ways! That being so, it is important that we discover the exact biblical meaning of the word because only then will we be in a position to understand its implications for us as Christians. We can trace the meaning of the word 'church' in three different ways.

*Firstly,* the original Greek word translated 'church' in our New Testament is *ekklesia,* which means a gathering together of people. Although widely adopted by the Christians (as we shall see throughout this chapter) it was not necessarily a religious word at all, but was often used to describe a democratic meeting of citizens to carry out lawful civic affairs. In Acts 19, for instance, we are told that when Paul's preaching caused a tremendous stir in the city of Ephesus, the town clerk told the people that any complaints against the Apostle would have to be dealt with 'in a legal assembly' (Acts 19:39) — and the word *'assembly'* is the Greek *ekklesia.*

*Secondly,* the Hebrew equivalent in the Old Testament is *qahal,* which comes from a root meaning 'to summon', and is sometimes translated 'assembly' in connection with the people of Israel. We are told, for instance, that 'the leaders of all the people of the tribes of Israel took their places in the *assembly* of the people of God' (Judges 20:2) and that Solomon blessed 'the whole *assembly* of Israel' (1 Kings 8:14); and the important thing to notice here is that the people were called together by God.

*Thirdly,* our English word 'church' — like the very similar Scottish word 'kirk' and the German 'kirche' — is derived from the Greek word *kuriakon,* an adjective meaning 'belonging to the Lord'. Now if we fuse these three strands together we have precisely the meaning the Bible intends us to have. The church is not a loose expression of religion in general, nor a group of professional leaders, nor a collection of bricks and mortar. To use an expanded paraphrase, the church is a gathering together of people called out by the Lord and belonging to him. All of this truth will now come through as we go on with our wider study of the subject.

## Living stones; a spiritual house

Although we have seen that the church is not to be thought of merely in terms of a collection of bricks and mortar, it is interesting to notice that the Bible *does* use building metaphors to describe it. Paul told the Christians at Corinth 'you are . . . God's building' (1 Corinthians 3:9) and a few verses later 'you are God's temple' (1 Corinthians 3:16), while he reminded the Christians at Ephesus that 'God's household' is 'built on the foundation of the apostles and prophets, with Christ Jesus himself as the chief corner-stone. In him the whole building is joined together and rises to become a holy temple in the Lord. And in him you too are being built together to become a dwelling in which God lives by his Spirit' (Ephesians 2:19—22). Peter took the same picture one step further and told the Christians to whom he wrote: 'As you come to (Christ) the living Stone —rejected by men but chosen by God and precious to him — you also, like living stones, are being built into a spiritual house' (1 Peter 2:4—5). The Bible *does* say that the church is a building, but it is a *spiritual* one, and the 'stones' used in its construction are 'living', men and women cemented by faith to the Lord Jesus Christ, the corner-stone who holds the whole building together.

## The holy bride

We are already getting more than a hint of the fact

that the Christian church is much more significant than most people think, and this becomes even clearer as we discover that it was specifically in order to redeem the church that Jesus came into the world. In the course of his teaching about being filled with the Spirit, Paul gives this instruction to married men — 'Husbands, love your wives, just as Christ loved the church and gave himself for her to make her holy, cleansing her by the washing with water through the word, and to present her to himself as a radiant church, without stain or wrinkle or any other blemish, but holy and blameless' (Ephesians 5:25—27).

In many passages in the Old Testament the Bible compares the relationship between God and his chosen people to that between a bridegroom and his bride — to give just one example, God tells the people of Israel 'For your Maker is your husband — the Lord Almighty is his name' (Isaiah 54:5) — and this is the picture which Paul is using here. When Jesus died on the cross it was not in the hope that some vague spiritual good might come about for the whole of mankind in general; it was for the specific purpose of releasing the church from sin and purchasing her to be his bride. The Bible clearly speaks of 'the church of God, which (Christ) bought with his own blood' (Acts 20:28). Now, 'by the washing with water through the word' (the progressive sanctification of believers by the application of God's word to their hearts and lives) he is preparing her for that great day when she will appear before him 'without stain or wrinkle or any other blemish, but holy and blameless'. Paul refers to this again when telling the Corinthians of his great concern for their spiritual and moral purity. He says 'I am jealous for you with a godly jealousy. I promised you to one husband, to Christ, so that I might present you as a pure virgin to him' (2 Corinthians 11:2). In today's world the church is often criticised, ridiculed or written off as irrelevant. But those who speak of the church in those terms could not be further from the truth. For all of its present faults and failures (and there are many) the church is nevertheless Christ's chosen bride, the object of his particular love, with an eternal future so glorious as to defy human imagination.

## One church only

For many years now there has been a great deal of discussion about what we could generally call 'church unity'. Councils and conferences and committees without number are working to bring the many different denominations closer together with the obvious final aim of uniting them in one world-wide organisation which would do away with all the other 'labels'. Now the whole subject of church unity, or the ecumenical movement is too vast to deal with in a brief study like this, but whatever may be right or wrong on the issue, we must never lose sight of the fact that *the true church is already united.* That may seem an extraordinary thing to say when there are so many hundreds of different denominations, sects and groupings of Christians — in one American city alone I was told that there were 27 varieties of Baptists! — but it remains a clear biblical fact. There is only one Christian church, what Paul calls 'the church of the living God' (1 Timothy 3:15), and it consists of every Christian in the world, past, present and future. Some of its members have not yet been born, some are living on the earth at the present time, and others died thousands of years ago! — but they are all united in *one church.* As Paul tells the Ephesians, 'There is one body and one Spirit — just as you were called to one hope when you were called — one Lord, one faith, one baptism; one God and Father of all, who is over all and through all and in all' (Ephesians 4:4—6).

## Visible and invisible

But even the very basic things we have noted so far raise some obvious questions. If the church is one, why are there so many denominations today? Are all members of local churches Christians? Are all Christians members of local churches? To answer the first question properly we would need to review the whole of church history, and we obviously cannot do that here, but in general terms we could say that most denominations came into being because people felt the need to emphasise particular aspects of Christian doctrine or practice, or to protest against current trends in the church at that time. But what of the other two questions? In order to answer them, it would be helpful if we thought of local congregations as 'the visible church' and of the sum total of all Christians throughout all ages as 'the invisible church' (in the sense that its essence is spiritual and not organisational). With those definitions in mind, we can now make two firm statements in answer to the questions.

### *Not all members of the visible church are members of the invisible church*

This is sadly but obviously true, as it was even in the early days of the Christian church. In Samaria, a magician by the name of Simon was baptized and identified himself with the local visible church, but when he offered to buy his way into a position of spiritual power Peter told him 'May your money perish with you, because you thought to buy the gift of God

with money! . . . your heart is not right before God
. . . you are full of bitterness and captive to sin'
(Acts 8:20—23). For a brief time at least, Simon was a
member of the visible church — people thought he
was a Christian — but the truth of the matter was that
he had never been truly born again. Association with
other Christians is no guarantee that a person is himself a true believer, nor is baptism, confirmation,
church membership or the holding of any ecclesiastical
office. In a passage describing the early growth of
Christianity we are told that 'the Lord added to their
number daily those who were being saved' (Acts 2:47)
— and not that the church added to the Lord! No
activity, ritual, ceremony, or pronouncement of the
church can ever make a person a Christian, and of
course this goes a long way towards explaining why
the visible church is such an unsatisfactory expression
of the invisible church. It is like a field of wheat
mixed with a rampant growth of weeds. In fact, this
is exactly the illustration Jesus used, and he added the
solemn warning that the day would come when he
would tell the reapers 'First collect the weeds and
tie them in bundles to be burned, then gather the
wheat and bring it into my barn' (Matthew 13:30).
The challenge of that statement is obvious!

*Not all members of the invisible church are members
of the visible church*

This is equally true — and equally sad! Some Christians,
and especially some young people, have become so
impatient with what they consider to be the failures of
the visible church that they have opted out of it
altogether. They have decided to go it alone, or to
meet with other like-minded Christians as and when
they feel like it, with no structure, discipline or con-

tinuing identity. Now the tragedy of that situation is that in trying to avoid frustration they have fallen into error. The Christian who does not identify with a local church is failing to follow the example of Jesus who 'on the Sabbath day . . . went into the synagogue as was his custom' (Luke 4:16); he is ignoring the later practice of the disciples, who met together 'on the first day of the week' (Acts 20:7); and he is flatly disobeying the Bible's clear instruction 'Let us not give up meeting together, as some are in the habit of doing, but let us encourage one another — and all the more as you see the Day approaching' (Hebrews 10:25). Whilst it is true that you do not become a Christian by going to church, it is equally true that you cannot be an obedient Christian while staying away! Every Christian has a responsibility to the Lord and to his fellow Christians to identify with a local church and to become thoroughly involved in its life, witness and ministry. Membership of a local church is not an optional extra for the Christian — it is a straightforward command to be obeyed. Ideally, your choice of a local church will be guided by a sincere belief that its doctrine, form of service and organisation are true to God's word. But do not hold back from joining a church just because in your view it is less than ideal in every one of these areas. Many a weak church has been given a new lease of life by spiritually-minded Christians willing to join it in a spirit of love and service. No local church is perfect — but there is no way in which it can ever be improved by the absence of spiritually-minded Christians!

## The New Testament way

Throughout these studies, we have kept firmly to one simple guideline — 'What does the Scripture say?'

(Romans 4:3) — and on the subject of the church the Scripture says a great deal. There is one passage in particular which will help us to see some of the marks of a New Testament church, and we shall end our studies by looking at it in detail. The passage opens on the Day of Pentecost, and reads as follows — 'Those who accepted (Peter's) message were baptized, and about three thousand were added to their number that day. They devoted themselves to the apostles' teaching and to the fellowship, to the breaking of bread and to prayer. Everyone was filled with awe, and many wonders and miraculous signs were done by the apostles. All the believers were together and had everything in common. Selling their possessions and goods, they gave to anyone as he had need. Every day they continued to meet together in the temple courts. They broke bread in their homes and ate together with glad and sincere hearts, praising God and enjoying the favour of all the people. And the Lord added to their number daily those who were being saved' (Acts 2: 41—47). From this fascinating glimpse of the early church, we can pick out seven clear identification marks, which ought ideally to be present in every local church today.

*Firstly, there should be worship*

In everything that they were doing, the members of the early church were 'praising God', and this is a distinguishing mark of any true church. In one of his great doxologies, Paul cries 'To (God) be glory in the church and in Christ Jesus throughout all generations, for ever and ever! Amen' (Ephesians 3:21). There is something seriously wrong whenever the emphasis in a local church is on the building, or the music, or the form of service, or even on any particular doctrine.

There is something equally wrong when there is an undue emphasis on the minister, with the result that the church becomes a preaching centre rather than a place of worship. When Christians attend their local church they should do so first and foremost in the spirit of the Psalmist who cried out 'Let us come before him with thanksgiving and extol him with music and song. . . . Come, let us bow down in worship, let us kneel before the Lord our Maker; for he is our God and we are the people of his pasture, the flock under his care' (Psalm 95:2, 6–7). And in joining together with other Christians in that way, they could have no greater incentive than the promise of the Lord Jesus himself, who said that 'where two or three come together in my name, there am I with them' (Matthew 18:20).

*Secondly, there should be sound doctrine*

We are told that those early Christians 'devoted themselves to the apostles' teaching', and this is a most important point to notice, because it speaks not only of doctrine, but of discipline. The new converts were not expected to learn the facts of the Christian faith by meeting in discussion groups, with one man's opinion carrying as much weight as the next. Instead, they gladly submitted to the God-given ministry of the apostles. Now there is obviously a place for discussion in the life of the church, but it should never take the place of the authoritative teaching of God's word by those called and equipped to give it. The Bible says 'Do not be carried away by all kinds of strange teachings' (Hebrews 13:9) – and the surest way to avoid error is to grow in the knowledge of the truth. Especially if you are young in the faith, acquire the happy discipline of learning from those who like

Apollos have 'a thorough knowledge of the Scriptures' (Acts 18:24). You will never regret it!

*Thirdly, there should be united prayer*
This is singled out as another distinguishing mark of the early church, and it is hardly surprising. Whilst we saw in an earlier chapter that a Christian may pray at any time and in any place, there is a particular value in Christians praying together. It was when 'many people had gathered and were praying' (Acts 12:12) that God worked in a miraculous way to release Peter from Herod's prison; and God still works in many mighty ways today in response to the united prayers of his people. To miss the place of united prayer is to miss where the action is!

*Fourthly, there should be the right administration of*
*    sacraments*
According to the New Testament, there are two sacraments binding on the Christian church, baptism and the .breaking of bread (otherwise known as The Lord's Supper or the Holy Communion) — and both are mentioned in the passage we are studying. We are told that 'those who accepted the message were baptised' and then that they 'devoted themselves to . . . the breaking of bread'. Both sacraments were instituted by Jesus himself, as 'the head of the church' (Ephesians 5:23). In sending the first disciples out on their world-wide mission he told them that they were to 'make disciples of all nations, baptizing them in the name of the Father and of the Son and of the Holy Spirit' (Matthew 28:19), and after sharing the bread and wine at his last evening meal with them, he said 'Do this in remembrance of me' (1 Corinthians 11:24—25). Baptism is an outward symbol of repentance and faith, a sign to

the world that the person baptised professes to trust
Christ as his Saviour and acknowledges him as his
Lord. The breaking of bread is a symbolic meal in
which Christians gratefully remind themselves that
their fellowship with God and with each other is based
entirely on Christ's death on their behalf. As Paul told
the Corinthians, 'For whenever you eat this bread and
drink this cup, you proclaim the Lord's death until he
comes' (1 Corinthians 11:26). Any local church seeking to base its practice on the New Testament will
include both of these sacraments, and individual
Christians seeking to be obedient to the Bible's teaching will gladly receive them.

### Fifthly, there should be warm-hearted fellowship

One of the greatest descriptions of the church in the
whole Bible is that it is 'the body of Christ' (1
Corinthians 12:27), a statement which vividly underlines its spiritual life and unity. But Paul adds, in
writing to the Christians at Rome, 'Just as each of us
has one body with many members, and these members
do not all have the same function, so in Christ we who
are many form one body, and *each member belongs to
all the others'* (Romans 12:4–5). Notice those last
words! In the deepest possible sense, Christians belong
to each other; they are joined together in the common
life that they draw from Christ – and they are meant
to show it by the sharing of that common life with
the other members of the church. A human body only
functions healthily when there is unrestricted circula-
tion of life-giving blood, and the church only functions
healthily when its members allow a free flow of their
spiritual life to circulate. When a Christian isolates
himself, he is cutting himself off from that which
would enrich his life, and he is holding back from

others that which would enrich theirs. Whatever the motives, that is both selfish and disobedient. In the New Testament, we read of Christians giving each other 'the right hand of fellowship' (Galatians 2:9) — not the cold shoulder!

## Sixthly, there should be mutual care

Notice how this comes through in our passage from Acts 2. We are told that 'All the believers were together and had everything in common. Selling their possessions and goods, they gave to anyone as he had need'. This follows on exactly from what we have just seen of the church as a body, with all the members interrelated. If you were to cut your hand, millions of white corpuscles would immediately rush through your bloodstream to the injured part in order to fight against infection, and in the sending of this help the brain, the nerves of the spinal column, the lungs and the intercostal breathing muscles will all have been involved. This marvellous co-operation takes place because the body is one; all of its members, to some degree or another, share both in its health and its sicknesses, or, as Paul puts it, 'If one part suffers, every part suffers with it; if one part is honoured, every part rejoices with it' (1 Corinthians 12:26). And what is true in the human body is meant to be true in the church. As Christians we should be identified by caring love and loving care. By our caring love we obey the Bible's command to 'Carry each other's burdens, and in this way you will fulfill the law of Christ' (Galatians 6:2), and by our loving care we obey the Bible's command to 'do good to all people especially to those who belong to the family of believers' (Galatians 6:10). The practice of better-off Christians selling their property and possessions in order to provide for the needs of the poor seems to have been limited to those very early days of the church in Jerusalem, but it is a vivid demonstration of the depth of fellowship they must have known. Let us see to it that nobody in our local church fellowship suffers from a need that we could and should meet. As John puts it, 'Dear children, let us not love with words or tongue but with actions and in truth' (1 John 3:18).

*Seventhly, there should be continuous evangelism*

Our passage ends with the words 'And the Lord added to their number daily those who were being saved' – and as 'faith comes from hearing the message, and the message is heard through the word of Christ' (Romans 10:17) this obviously means that the church was continuously engaged in evangelism. No church is obedient that is not evangelistic. Not every service or meeting held in a church will be specifically aimed at the unconverted, of course, but throughout its children's work, its young people's programme, the normal activities of the church on Sundays and during the week, and perhaps from time to time in special events, the straightforward message of the Gospel will come through loud and clear. People will be faced with the fact of their sin, the danger of their condition, the love of God, the death and resurrection of Christ, the need for conversion, the brevity of life, the certainty of death, and the reality of judgment. Nor will the ideal church's concern be limited to its own locality or country; its vision will be world-wide and it will do all it can to help in the work of overseas missionary enterprise, sharing in the tremendous task of taking the gospel 'to the ends of the earth' (Acts 1:8).

How does your church measure up to that picture? Or, to be more personal, how would you measure up to being a member of such a church? No honest Christian can evade the questions — and most know the answers! David ended one of his Psalms with the words 'Search me, O God, and know my heart; test me and know my anxious thoughts. See if there is any offensive way in me and lead me in the way everlasting' (Psalm 139:23—24). You could have no better prayer as you end this book and continue learning and living the Christian life!